FIRE Burning Within

Fiercely Taking on Life to Achieve Victory
with God Leading You Every Step of the Way

Dan Jason

authorHOUSE

AuthorHouse™
1663 Liberty Drive
Bloomington, IN 47403
www.authorhouse.com
Phone: 1 (800) 839-8640

© *2020 Dan Jason. All rights reserved.*

No part of this book may be reproduced, stored in a retrieval system, or transmitted by any means without the written permission of the author.

Published by AuthorHouse 06/01/2020

ISBN: 978-1-7283-6322-6 (sc)
ISBN: 978-1-7283-6320-2 (hc)
ISBN: 978-1-7283-6321-9 (e)

Library of Congress Control Number: 2020909893

Print information available on the last page.

Any people depicted in stock imagery provided by Getty Images are models, and such images are being used for illustrative purposes only.
Certain stock imagery © Getty Images.

This book is printed on acid-free paper.

Because of the dynamic nature of the Internet, any web addresses or links contained in this book may have changed since publication and may no longer be valid. The views expressed in this work are solely those of the author and do not necessarily reflect the views of the publisher, and the publisher hereby disclaims any responsibility for them.

Contents

Dedication ix
Acknowledgments xi
Foreword: (Rick Jason) xiii

CHAPTER 1: Igniting the Flame 1
CHAPTER 2: God is for Us, Not Against Us 9
CHAPTER 3: Rebound 15
CHAPTER 4: Entering the Game 37
CHAPTER 5: Dancing with the Devil 48
CHAPTER 6: Glimmer of Light 61
CHAPTER 7: From Death to Resurrection 68
CHAPTER 8: Nunc Coepi 79
CHAPTER 9: Change the Channel 83
CHAPTER 10: Starting Lineups 93
CHAPTER 11: Radiant Future 101
CHAPTER 12: Run Your Own Race 114
CHAPTER 13: Discipline to Rise Above the Tide.................119
CHAPTER 14: Extreme Leadership & Extreme
               Accountability 133
CHAPTER 15: Vamanos 144
CHAPTER 16: Forgiveness..149
CHAPTER 17: The Little Things 156
CHAPTER 18: Step out of the Boat 164
CHAPTER 19: Wild & Free 180
CHAPTER 20: Gracias 186
CHAPTER 21: Power of Prayer & Divine Connection 193
CHAPTER 22: Final Shot 215

CHAPTER 23: Living the Dream 219
CHAPTER 24: Claim Your Crown 225

Author's Note 233
Scripture for Encouragement..235
References 239

To everyone out there not knowing how they will make it. Keep rising and grinding every day. Keep the faith, take the next step, and know you have what it takes to capture the life you desire.

Dedication

This book is dedicated to my Uncle Jim, Aunt Linny, and anyone out there who is battling and dealing with great adversity. Know that you are loved and your positive attitude, determination, grit, and fighting spirit motivates me every day. Your love and the way that you approach life, no matter what is thrown your way is inspiring. You are the true heros, the very people who get up and get after it. Despite all the cards stacked against you, you grind daily with a smile on your face and in doing so you shine brightly in this world. It is amazing to witness the tenacity by which you live by and the attitude you have. You look the odds right in the eyes and decide each morning that you will win the day. You stare down positivity and continue to dream big. Nothing will stop you, as love, faith, and hope is your battle cry. You have taught me so much, more than you could ever know. It is people like you who make the world a better place and leave their mark in a profound way on the generations to come. Thank you for encouraging me by living a life filled with faith, trust, bravery, and boldness. Your thirst for life is contagious. You deal with all of the challenges you encounter with great humility and never complain. Your heart is full of gratitude and you embody a winning persona that gives wings to your family and those around you. Champions you are, and champions you forever will be. May God bless you and may you stay strong and continue to fight the good fight!

Love,
Dan

Acknowledgments

I was first introduced to writing a book when I met my wife over a decade ago. She was an English major when we studied at Le Moyne College and a real go getter. She sparked an interest in me and explained the importance of telling one's story, as well as listening to the stories of others. Motivation has always been something I have tapped into. My goals, dreams, and aspirations in life, like yours, are important. During my lifetime I have read a number of inspirational books, many of which have lit a spark or reignited my faith. These great works of literature have enkindled my desire to become better and have sparked greatness that lies inside. The books and pieces of literature I have read were much more than mere words on a page. There are millions of books out there. People take months, even years, to formulate their ideas and put them down on paper. Then, after a long and arduous process, their work materializes and becomes something we can read. Like many, I believe that knowledge is power. I believe that it is a key that can unlock great doors, stimulate creativity, fill people with hope, enkindle an appetite for progress, and move us toward what we desire.

As for me, I chose to write this particular book because everyone has a story. In each of our lives we go through some unexplainable things that teach us a lot. There are victories and there are defeats. There are ups and there are downs. There are joyous moments and there are moments that suck the very life out of us. Being human and walking on this planet is a great privilege and yet it can be one of the most challenging things. We have our quintessential "good" days for lack of a better term and our moments that drag us down to the pit of despair. Then there are many moments that find a way to fit in between.

I am grateful to have had the opportunity to write this book. I wanted to share with you some of the powerful stories from my life, what I have learned along the way, and what has inspired me to become better. My desire was to create a work that encompasses personal narrative as well as motivation so that you too will be able to overcome and conquer during your life's journey. I greatly appreciate everyone who has helped me with this writing process and all of those who have encouraged me along the way. My hope is that you will be able to relate to my story, utilize the advice and inspirational thoughts that I have compiled, and tap into the fire that burns within you to live your best life. I am excited to embark on this adventure with you and hope that it encourages you to reflect upon your own life so that you may grow and become the best version of yourself. My motivation and wish is that inasmuch as life has taken me for a wild ride, that you too will be open to God and allow Him to stoke the fire of your heart. In doing so I believe that your life can be forever changed and you will be able to live your best life, becoming all you were created to be. It is my desire that you are inspired and galvanized by something that I have shared through my words and that you are able and willing to yield your own testimony, sharing your life experiences with others.

As we know, everyone wants to be heard and human connection is a key and essential component to a fulfilled life. Relationships are what we need and what we crave. Most of all, we need a relationship with the One who created us. God is an essential ingredient for our lives and He desires to enter in. When we trust and allow Him to direct our paths, He can set the entire course of our lives ablaze with new hope, new life, and new purpose. Our Lord and God desires us to be happy and fulfilled. We deserve to have an internal joy and to experience life to the fullest potential, tapping into who we truly are. By unmasking ourselves, by trusting, and walking by faith, it is my hope that through this book you come to fully understand that His love is never failing. You were meant for greatness and the fire inside of you is ready to flare up with great ferocity. God bless you and may the Lord carry you through everything with his amazing and abundant grace. May the love of Christ be upon you and your family both now and forever. It is time to shine and time for you to take the crown of life and victory which is yours!

-Dan Jason

Foreword

Going All In

He sat at the table, eyes glaring at him. Everyone wondered what move he would make. Shades on, a stoic demeanor on his face, he was ready to play his hand. The cards had been dealt at the beginning of the game and he now put his entire stack of chips on the table. It was time to seize the moment and go all in. Like a poker player, life deals us a deck without discretion. Some of the cards are great and others in our hand can be quite poor. How we play the hand is totally up to us. Regardless of what the dealer, namely life, dishes out to us, we must be willing to put all of our chips on the table. In order for us to crush it and win in life, we must go ALL IN!

Inside all of us exists something else, an X-factor, another gear. When we tap into this force it will cause an explosion in our lives. There is an internal motivation that lays deep within. A fire that is inside all of us. We can allow it to lay dormant or we can tap into it and be ignited. The Spirit, the Creator, the Lord of the Universe is living within us and wants to be infused in our lives in such a way that will ignite our path to new potential and dynamic possibilities.

Everything in life has a price. We must decide what we are willing to spend or what we will put our chips on to find our crowns that are out there. Each one of us has been blessed with time, talents, and treasure. We have the opportunity to use what we have been given to serve others and to share with the world what we have inside. How we use the hand we have been dealt is up to us. We are defined by our character, the mental and moral qualities that are distinctive to an individual. When God is with us and we allow him to enter our lives, we have everything we need. No matter what life deals us, good cards or bad, we will be well equipped to overcome and chase down victory. This is the beginning toward overcoming the odds and finding your crown in life.

Who is the rock that one may build a strong house upon? A solid foundation will set one up for success in every aspect of life. This foundation will not be shaken when life grows hard or obstacles come our way. We begin by recognizing that we are not in control of our lives and yet we are not alone. We must strive to become holy. Christ desires to live within us and wants to walk with us so His power can transform us. Our crowns are patiently waiting for us to claim. It is important to understand that we are all entrusted with individual gifts which come from above and that life is out there for our taking.

We each face trials and will encounter troubles at different times in our lives. These trials if approached with real strength can lead us to look to God rather than to this world for comfort and understanding. Suffering is part of life and is inevitable. God feels our pain. If life was easy and without suffering, we would not need God. Suffering is what brings us back to Him and allows us to build character, perseverance, and faith. The strength we gain by tapping into that fire within is what ignites our lives as we strive for greatness.

Only God knows why the good and the bad occur in our lives as He is our creator. One's life is a gift from above. It is for this very reason why it is so important for people to be "all in" when it comes to their approach to life and their relationship with God. To be "all in" requires faith. Faith is our belief, complete trust and confidence in God and His promise to us. This promise takes root beginning with our faith which leads to happiness. Happiness is not measured in the abundance of the things we possess. Happiness results from being grateful with who we are, what we have, and where we are going. Perfect love casts out all fear, doubt, and darkness. When we are true to ourselves and accept the burning love that God has for us we will be led to happiness and joy. To grow in love and happiness we must turn our backs on fear and trust God completely. By establishing an intimate relationship with Him through prayer and by tapping into our passions, we take the first step to being "all in" and live an authentic life.

Humans are either Being or Becoming. Like mirrors, we are either revealing God's love and light through our own lives and to the world or we are blinding others with our own self-interests and ego. Ultimately, the latter will destroy our very selves, while the former will lead us to uncover the crowns that await us. When in the Spirit and "all in," God's fire burns inside us. Trust in God and do good and He shall bring it to pass. He who lives in love, lives in God. As Saint Francis of Assisi stated, "For it is in giving that we receive God's grace from above."

Is there a Fire that burns within? If one is contemplating this question one has begun to discover the path that God has opened up for him or her here on this Earth. Believe and achieve greatness. This is one of many tenets that a Man of God I know so well, lives by. I was asked by my son Dan to write the Forward to this book about discovering deep within oneself the fire and faith that will help us overcome life's challenges and launch us into our ultimate destiny. At an early age, we began to call Dan by the nickname "Dan-the-Man." Dan loved to be around family members and living in the moment on *The Hill* where he grew up.. He earned this nickname due to his maturity, passion when engaging in an activity, and his concern for others. These attributes continued to develop which helped shape and define Dan's character of steadfast faith, love, respect, strength, integrity, humility, and compassion. It is all of these attributes that has enabled Dan to take a leap of faith each time trusting in God as he forges ahead in search of another crown of glory.

Dan's approach to life begins with the question, "What would Jesus do?" This question has helped Dan navigate his journey in life, overcome great odds, and become the best version of himself that he aspires to be. Dan majored in Religious Studies at LeMoyne College in Syracuse, NY intending to become a priest thereafter. During discernment he felt that he was being led to become an elementary educator and worked with inner-city children, taking a job in Albany, New York. Dan became a male role model for many students during the next eight years of his teaching tenure. While a freshman in college, Dan became the manager of the Dolphins basketball team. It was during this time that Dan underwent a transformation of body, and began to workout with an intense regiment. His dedication to training continued each year enabling him to build strength and stamina. The external power he developed, pales in comparison to the inward fortitude he has built up over the years in constantly seeking out God's will for his life. A real example of *being* and *becoming*, striving to embody the best version of himself. At the beginning of his Senior year, Dan, a former walk on, was named the team captain, evident of his leadership on and off the court.

Living with discipline is an ideal Dan exemplifies in his everyday life. He is thankful for all that he has and is humble at heart. Dan enjoys service work and giving back to those in need. He avidly volunteers his time at the Rescue Mission in Albany, leading bible studies at the Coxsackie Prison, and serving as a missionary with Hope of the Poor and Baseball Miracles in places like Mexico City and other areas of destitute poverty around the world. He has discovered the flame and fire that burns within himself, which has led him to love the poor, sharing his concern and hope for God's people. Dan continues to amaze our family with his abounding energy to write a book in order to help others take a hard look at where they are in their life journey and the untapped potential they have. When I think of Dan, I see holiness, seeing with the eyes of Christ, trusting God, and letting go of one's ego and fear. Our work each day is only an expression of the love we have for God.

What does it require for one to be "all in" and to claim one's crown in order to find treasure in life? It requires one to do his or her personal best. One must be willing to stay the course by making a commitment, exhibiting discipline and sticking to it regardless of circumstances or hardship. It requires making the right choice and continuing to trust. Lastly, it requires passion in all that one does, which will sustain one through good times and help one cope during difficult situations. One's passion will shine as a beacon of light and inspire others. This challenge is for each of us. It is time to choose between *being* or *becoming*. We each have been created for greater things. We were created to love others as God loves us. I invite you to join Dan on this journey and to become the greatest version of yourself in order to live a full and authentic life.

My dad has taught me a lot in life, especially how to be fully committed, accountable, and to give 100% in all I do.

"The fire inside people is like a match: the way to ignite that flame is initially through friction, then other matches are lit through warmth."

-Stephen R. Covey

CHAPTER 1: Igniting the Flame

When you strike a match it takes friction and force to create the spark. Within a few seconds there is fire. That fire can be extinguished quickly or it may be fed and fueled in order to grow and burn. Fire is one of the most valuable resources on this planet. The first humans, including cavemen tens of thousands of years ago, found this life changing element made of heat and created by force. This ball of intense energy would ultimately change the game for creation. Fire is the very substance that allows us to have light in order to see in the darkness. It provides humankind with warmth to brave the cold and survive the frigid months of winter. Fire is accessed and used daily across the globe as the method to cook food and fuel our bodies to be well nourished. Fire is a necessity and a commodity that was an asset millennia ago and remains as one of the most treasured renewable resources planet earth has to offer. It is evident that we, human beings, absolutely cannot live without it. Yet, with it, we do much much more than survive...We thrive!

    I remember back to when I was just five years old and I popped out of bed like a piece of toast. I woke up so excited because today was my birthday! Oh yeah and it wasn't going to be just any birthday party, I was going to have the best party ever with all of my friends there. My birthday that year was going to be cowboy themed. Back in the day as a little kid I might as well have been John Wayne. It was the wild west in my house from sunup to sun down. A ten gallon hat on my head, plaid shirt, handkerchief and bola around my neck. I had a big leather belt with a huge buckle and of course cowhide chaps that went over my denim jeans. Big black leather boots finished off my get up and a holster on each side of my hip with my six shooter pistol. Nobody would be messing with me because I was locked and loaded ready for any villains who might be coming through town. Everyone was impressed with my outfit, they didn't know that this was how I dressed every day after school and on the weekends. As the guests poured in dressed in their finest cowboy and cowgirl attire, the mountain of presents grew higher and higher. I could smell the cake baking in the oven and was super excited to get this party started. Country western music was bumping in the background and drinks were flowing for the grownups like it was a real saloon. It was time for me to take the center stage and the singing of *Happy Birthday.* My dad took out the matches and with one swift stroke light the first candle, followed by four more. Five candles burning brightly on top of my homemade cowboy cake. I could almost taste the warm chocolate and sweet vanilla frosting. The light from those candles glowed and the flames danced in the air, swaying from side to side. This is my first memory not only of my birthday that I can remember, but also fire. One small spark of energy. Yellow with a tinge of orange, producing light. After the birthday song, I closed my eyes and made a wish. I don't remember what my exact wish was, but I do remember asking my dad later on that night an important question. Dad, "How is fire created?" I was in awe of the flame and couldn't understand it. One second it was not there, then it was glowing and burning. My dad said, "Well you see Dan, it is created by a force called friction and heat to create energy." Amazing stuff. Somethings you don't forget, the fire and flame was something that was burnt into my memory. I now realize why.

At age five I was ready to Cowboy up for a wild wild west Birthday party!

Fire is energy, and within each and every fire there is a flame. You are alive, breathing, and your existence has great power. There is a flame inside of you. When you tap into that flame, when you find that divine spark and forcefield and come to know what it is that drives and motivates you, your life changes remarkably. It is at that moment of personal discovery within your being that a new spark is ignited and begins to burn fiercely. Often we need to dump a little fuel on the fire or put some extra wood on it to rev it up and get it going. Life tends to provide events, experiences, and ways of igniting us. The friction we face in our lives serves as the driftwood to allow our personal fire to burn and grow. Fire, if it is neglected or left alone, will eventually die out. Such is true with us and our lives. If we do not stay hungry, driven, motivated, and connected to positive and life giving people, initiatives, and endeavors, we too will someday fizzle out. As Chad Kellog once said, "The story you tell yourself becomes your reality." So what do you want that reality to be? What is your story? It is time to write the best part, it is time to become fully alive!

Do not sit back and allow your life to merely pass by. We cannot live a life of apathy or passivity. There is far too much at stake and we must not risk being a mere ember in life. Instead, we must turn inwardly, as we have within each of us, all that is necessary to burn with unquenchable force. Your time is now, not tomorrow or later on. Today is the day to embrace the anthem, "Burn baby burn!" Your fire is waiting on the inside and is one match away from reigniting. You have everything necessary at your disposal to alter your personal density. You can blaze a trail for yourself, while singing a lifelong impact on those who journey with you.

As I write this book amidst the very epicenter of the Coronavirus pandemic that has tightened its grip and put the clamps on every society in dramatic fashion around our world, we need to reignite the spark and flame as a society. People around the globe have been impacted in a tremendous way. Millions of members of the human family have become gravely sick, hundreds of thousands have died, and billions are now confined to quarantine or are isolated from the rest of society in order to stop the spread through social distancing.

I believe this is the universe giving us a prime opportunity to be personally reignited and as a world to be fired up. As we know, life is short so what better time than now and who better to do it than you and me. We have nothing to lose, yet everything to gain.

This entire whirlwind of a situation in this crazed era we now live in has taught us well that life is fragile. What we consume, what we focus our time and energy on is critical because there are no guarantees. Time is of an essence and for some people who have grown ill during this period in history, that time is quickly running out. For most of us in society, eventually the dust will settle and things will indeed get back to normal. The economic crisis we are facing amidst the chaos and shutdown of the majority of society will erect itself and reverse taking an upswing in the future. People will no longer be required to stay confined to their homes. We will all go back to work and schools will be reopened. churches and congregations will be able to practice as a community once again and we will be permitted to reconnect person to person. Businesses will be pushed forward and the world will eventually get back on track.

Yet, will the masses have learned a valuable lesson from these trying times? I do not mean will we have learned how to better prepare for the next health crisis or pandemic. Although that is important, I hope that we as a nation in the United States and the world for that matter, have taken the time that was provided to us during this great shutdown to have reflected on life, and deciphered the meaning of it. Slowing down can be quite the blessing and can allow for us to understand what is most important. Where do we fit into this universal equation? In addition, have we prioritized things, thought about our past, and contemplated who we are as individuals. Do we understand better what we have faced and have we created a more decisive and clear plan for where we want to go. Do we know who we want to become? This is a moment of truth. What is your life's value and how will you utilize each day you are blessed with?

Ultimately, each individual has a choice and we will go one of two ways. The flame within us will either gain power and be set ablaze, roaring into the future with great promise and purpose. Or that light that glows within will dissipate and be quenched by fear, doubt, disbelief, laziness, blame, and feelings of insufficiency. The same God who gifted each of us the spark of life, and every breath that pours into our lungs, will be there for us and with us one way or another. The path we choose is totally up to us. It is time to be set ablaze!

It is my hope that a divine spark is singed on our very hearts that we might approach life differently. Our time and focus should be on conquering the things that are trying to hold us down, on overcoming the hardship, the iniquities, and the struggles we face. We must do this for ourselves and we must do this for those around us. It is time for us as a human community to band together and unite. It is time for us to bond and share our light. Now is the time for us to ignite. What we desire is very much the same; food, water, shelter, love, respect, acceptance, and community.

The dog eat dog world we live in is not getting anyone anywhere. So long as there are billions of flames burning independently and in and of themselves, unity and fire will not grow. One by one when we come together, tell our story and listen to others, the flame of hope will grow brighter. It is in these very moments that the flame of love, one person at a time, will grow stronger, and the light will dispel the darkness because it will be far too powerful and bright. There is a reason why we are where we are as a society and nation. The real pandemic is not in the form of COVID-19. The real pandemic we face is a lack of faith, a reduction of unity, straying away from family, an absence of peace, a decrease of communion, an insufficiency of truth, and a shortage of inner strength.

The fire that burns inside of you and the fire that burns inside of me, the very fame of faith and the flame of hope can be what changes our world. The first step is to conquer and overcome our own trials and challenges. We must ignite the fire in our personal lives so we can burn to our fullest potential. Each of us faces mountains and we can either stare at them and give up or put on our climbing gear and start the ascent. Then when we get to the top we will have accomplished something great. Nevertheless, that is not the end point, as it is critical that we don't merely stay up there, but we support and aid those who are also trudging through, on the rise of the climb.

St. Ignatius of Loyola knew about the fire that burns within the human person very well. Many years before he came to prominence, Ignatius was out on the battlefield during the battle of Pamalonia in 1521. As a member of the military he fought and gave his all for his French nation. Unfortunately, Ignatius was severely injured as his leg was shattered to smithereens and he could fight no more. He could have quit. He could have very easily given up and thrown in the towel. After all, who would have blamed him, he had a sure way out. There was something within that young man, something that was embedded deep down at the core. There was a fire waiting to be set ablaze. While in the hospital and recovering from his injuries, there were two options of books for Ignatius to read, *Romances of Chivalry*, and *The Life of Jesus and Lives of the Saints*. Ignatius, being a contemplative in his day, began to read both. Soon thereafter, he turned the majority of his focus and attention to the latter, which would lead ultimately to his conversion. Little did Ignatius know that he would soon be joined by other great men of faith in the likes of Peter Favre and St. Francis Xavier. These men took what was a horrific time in their lives to band together and form what is today known as the Society of Jesus, namely The Jesuits. For as, "Iron sharpens iron, so does one man sharpen another." (Proverbs 27:17)

During times of despair and what looks like defeat, we too have the opportunity to come together to set the world ablaze and to change the course of history. This happens one day, one person, and one encounter at a time. Will you be the igniter and keep the fire burning? Or will you let it blow out or worse, put it out. As Ignatius is such a powerful example of taking a set back and turning it into a set up, we have the opportunities to do just the same in our own way. We all face things that can be negative and draining, yet we can find a way to deal with them and allow God to turn those trials into some more positive over the course of time. In doing so we will change the trajectory of our life. If Ignatius can do this, so too can you and I. The time has come and this generation needs us. Ignatius said it best, "Now go out and set this world on fire!"

"You have to believe in yourself and you have to believe in the people who believe in you."

-Tim Tebow

CHAPTER 2: God is for Us, Not Against Us

There have been innumerable occasions in my life where I have experienced God. He is omnipresent when waking up to a warm sunny day, sitting on a picnic table with my great grandfather while watching some deer graze in a meadow, or catching my Godson who races and jumps into my arms. God is present and his presence is felt. Most of the time it is a matter of opening up our eyes to His goodness and His subtlety that permeates our lives on a regular basis so long as we are aware of it. There are also some amazing moments where God appears and is felt in a profound way. These are often much easier to notice and leave a stronger and deeper imprint in our memories. Meanwhile, life has a ton of what we have defined to be ordinary or average moments. These are often times in our lives where we can say that God was there, as He is always by our side. And still yet, there are times when we are scared, bruised, and battered, life taking a turn for the worst. Was God there with us through those moments? How did we carry on?

This is what I believe. I believe that God is truly for us and not against us. He created us out of his own kindness and care. We came into being out of God's personal choice. He gave us life, not because He needs us, but because He loves us. When we realize that there is nothing that we can do to earn God's love nor anything that can separate us from His everlasting love, our lives will be changed. It is the very promise of life in Jesus Christ that keeps me going every single day. The promise of the Lord's love and redemptive power are what kept me alive and going during my darkest moments, as I battled through hell on earth. Some of the things that I will share with you in this book will be tough pills to swallow. There are stories in here that will inevitably shake you to the core. You will read some things that will indeed blow your mind and make you question life itself. The reason why I decided to hold nothing back and not water down the content of what is included in this book is because life in all of its form is real. Nothing about life is diluted and the truth is necessary to set us free. The personal testimony and pieces I have decided to unveil and speak about are not to scare you or alarm you. Instead, these parts of my journey that I share are to help you understand that everyone has a story and that we all face difficulty. It is in the midst of that turmoil, when we are at the end of our rope and are full of despair that we can cry out to God for help and the Lord will carry us through it all.

I cannot imagine how anyone moves through life without faith or knowing Christ. It seems impossible to me to be able to wake up every day and go after things, even the good, without the support and love of the Lord. It is unfathomable for me to comprehend trying to overcome some of the gravest things that we human beings face on our own without divine assistance.

Society will often feed us negative thoughts. Why try anyway? Aren't we going to face more challenges and obstacles along the way? Won't new barriers appear? Life in one regard can be very daunting; however, when we realize that each triumph over darkness, each victory over the odds is actually what makes us stronger, we grow and we glow! We are refined by the fires we blaze through and our soul grows in magnificence and strength. Every time we carry on and heed the battle cry that says, "I will not give up, I must not give up, I can, and I will," we burn stronger.

During my three decades on this planet the most profound thing I have learned is that every day is a blessing. Everyday is an opportunity to improve, discover who we are, and strive toward what we want to accomplish. The future is uncertain and the past cannot be changed; however, the way we approach life is essential. When we have the right mindset, the power of positivity, and most importantly a real steadfast faith that we can cling to then nothing can stop us and we will win!

See, God doesn't desire bad things to happen or curses to come upon us in our lives. Yet, life throws us curve after curve and sometimes the fastball we cannot catch up to. Life is hard, really

really hard, and we go through so much. Occasionally we break down and every so often we want to quit and just throw in the towel because we have had enough. But when we keep plowing through, when we stay the course and dig our heels in during the messy and exhausting times, our character grows.

Life may pull us back and stretch us so damn far in the opposite direction, but God has a way to use that immense amount of tension to launch us into our destiny. Remember, we serve a God who has no bounds. As pastor Joel Osteen so often reminds his congregation, God raised Jesus from the grave and the same resurrection power is in us through his Holy Spirit. If you just have faith the size of a mustard seed you will see the magnanimous ways that God can and will work in your life. He will guide you through things you never thought possible and take you to places you could have never dreamt of.

The key is to trust. The main thing is to keep standing and keep that fire alive. Remember the words of the prophet Jeremiah, "For I know the plans I have for you says the Lord. Plans to prosper you, not to harm you, plans to give you hope and a future." (Jeremiah 29:11) God created you and me with only good in mind and that He desires us to not only have a good life here on earth, but the best in Heaven for all eternity. Unfortunately, life does not only have good in it, and there are bad times that will come our way. So how can St. Paul write, "All things work together for good for those who love God." (Romans 8:28) What does he mean? The man who had arguably the most profound conversion in history when it comes to relationship with God, was trying to tell us something really valuable. St. Paul went from being the lead persecutor of Christans and trying to at all costs kill those who practiced the faith, to the most loving and dedicated man of God who wrote two thirds of the New Testament. St. Paul understands to the fullest that God will bring us through anything we face and work it for the good. He shows us by his example that in the end God will use what seemed like it was meant to harm us, to lead us to become better and stronger. The fire rages within and we become an inspiration to the world!

Every battle we face provides an opportunity to tackle what is before us. We have a choice to make each day when our eyes open and we are gifted another shot at life. As Eric Thomas so prolifically explained, life boils down to a choice. Eric explained that in life we can be one of two animals, we either decide to become the Lion or we choose to be the Gazelle. He goes on to say that on the Savanna, the sun rises every day. Life at its essence is made up of pretty simple things. You can choose life or you can choose death. You can either choose to be the Lion or the Gazelle. Now both animals run and they can move fast on the open plain. Each species was designed to sprint and has power within itself to maneuver quickly when it decides to go. Yet, a major difference exists between the Lion and the Gazelle just like a major difference exists between a blazing fire and a little ember. Gazelles are constantly running from things, as they are always scared and running away. Every day, every time danger comes, the Gazelle continues to run away and eventually it is chased down and eaten. But Lions are beasts. Lions on the other hand, are the King of the jungle. Lions are always going after what they desire and know what they want. Even when it's difficult to find their prey, the Lion continues to pursue it. When a drought ensues and the animals they feast on leave for a new land, the Lion chases down and devours its prey. The Lion aggressively assaults the challenge through its relentlessness. It is not owned by anything or anyone, but instead the Lion decides to attack.

In life when resistance comes our way or detrimental circumstances come about, we must not sit back and say, "why me, this isn't fair." We must look ourselves in the mirror, understand what we were created for and most importantly who created us. We must attack. When we have goals and ambitions, when we have desires burning in our hearts, we must not run away afraid like the Gazelle. No, we must become a beast. We must embody the Lion and track that thing down!

We must also know and always remember that "No weapon formed against me shall prosper." (Isaiah 54:17) We have God on our side and instead of telling people and ourselves how big our problems are, we must start telling our issue how big our God is. Pastor Osteen reminds us of the grand essence of the Lord and that God can take anything and be able to use it to bring us closer to Him. In the end God uses the struggle and the friction in our lives to make us stronger. For our God is for us, not against us. No matter what cards are dealt to us in the game of life, remember that with God on our side we will overcome and be victorious. Go out there and claim your crown. Be a Lion and be a beast.

CHALLENGE #1: When has God been for you?

The first challenge is for you to reflect and pray on where and when God has been for you in your life. Maybe it was a time you could remember long ago. Or perhaps something more recently happened and you knew that God had a hand in it. Jot down your thoughts in a journal and begin keeping track of "God Moments," the times when God showed up and showed out in your life and you know He was for you.

"Resilience is knowing that you are the only one that has the power and the responsibility to pick yourself up."

-Mary Halloway

CHAPTER 3: Rebound

How would life go on? He was gone now and would not be coming back. Nothing could change this situation. It was unfair. Confusion, hurt, and sorrow filled his aching heart. Why had this happened? Why, if you really loved us, would you allow such horrible things to transpire? How could this be? It is unimaginable and yet it is his reality. It might be yours as well. Have you or someone you deeply love ever felt this way before? If so, you are not alone. Life has a tendency at times to drag us down. If we are not careful, we can fall into a pit of despair which may be difficult to climb or find our way back out. Bouncing back after a setback in life is hard. Being able to rebound after a loss, grief, disappointment, or some other defeat is not easy. Nevertheless, finding the resolve within to do so is key if you are to live your best life. If you fall down, fail, or get knocked off track, as challenging as it may be, just get back up again and keep going. So long as you stand when you get hit and tumble to the floor, so long as you do not stay down and out, you will be able to rebound from whatever it is that is trying to steal your joy. Like a boxer on the ropes in a prize fight, you have to find the fire within, the wherewithal to have the guts and grit to not back down. You have a champion inside and you are a winner, so get back up. The only person that can stop you, is you!

Growing up with a younger brother and a ton of cousins was a lot of fun. We would spend countless hours playing outside on the swingset, swimming in the pool on hot summer days, and building gigantic snow forts during the winter time. My cousins and I rode bikes all over our family's property, chasing after one another. At night time we would engage in some really intense games of manhunt and launching the toboggan down the huge hill up and over a massive jump was exhilarating. With most things we did we had teams, kept score, and competition was always running high. Something I always struggled with since I was a young child is getting over things, especially defeat. Whether it was competition with my cousins out in the yard, a game or sport I played, or an assignment I completed for a grade in school, I struggled with setbacks. The relentlessness and drive for "perfection" I had at such a young age was my greatest asset and at times, my biggest detriment. Understanding how to harness that fire in the right direction is essential. When things didn't go according to plan or if I didn't do as well as I expected it was disastrous. My entire world crumbled. It was as if I became a puddle and everyone began to step on me. I was stuck in the mud. Let alone, if I lost or there was a sudden change in my life situation like a death in the family, forget it. I would sink so far down into a rabbit hole, it was like sliding into the unknown world of Alice in Wonderland. The main problem was, there was no wonderland and Alice was eating me up on the inside. It took many years for me to stop beating myself up and wearing all of my emotions and feelings on my sleeve. I took things hard and was not willing to accept failure at anything, even if it wasn't in my control. The problem was, back in those days, I would sulk, cry, and try to run away from the problems or setbacks. Now, I realize that rebounding in life is all about being on the offensive, verses constantly playing defense. Bouncing back requires guts and it also means that we are progressive verses merely reactive toward difficult situations. No is perfect nor will we ever be, however that doesn't mean we can't strive for perfection and give our best especially after a loss.

At age 9, I won the east regional of the *Elks National Hoop Shoot* and went on to take 6th place overall in NY State.

As Stephen Richards said best, "The true measure of success is how many times you can bounce back from failure." We walk this road of life and there is so much that is out of our control. Every single day of our lives we wake up and by the days end, our hearts continue to need healing. Life is hard, it is really really hard. There are countless impingements on our lives that cause us frustration on a daily basis; however, some events and circumstances in life are unavoidable and can really cause our hearts to hurt, driving a very knife into the core of our souls. When you lose a loved one, when a spouse walks out, when your child goes off the deep end, or when the future is taken from you, it makes you question God. Why do bad things happen to good people?

For centuries upon centuries, humanity has wondered this and even the most devout and faith filled people have remained puzzled by this predicament. Why does an all loving God of the Universe allow tragic events and evil to hurt us? We may never know the exact answer to this age old question until we reach the other side of the gates of Heaven; however, it doesn't take away the agony or the grief. Our pain is real, it exists, and it lasts. A snap of a finger, a sudden breakthrough, or some other quick fix will not and cannot erase that agony and heartache that has welled up inside. Within us, that torment will eat us up and suck all the life out of us if we are not careful and we do not seek ways to heal. It is a dark and dangerous path that must be avoided at all costs. As difficult as it may be, we must find a way to get back on track and retain a positive mindset. Remember, where there is a will, there is a way.

During the 17th Century, the world was struck by the Plague. As our world suffers during this pandemic that we now face head on with Coronavirus, we face similar uncertainty. Someone we could learn from perhaps is Sir Isaac Newton. In his hometown, just outside of the city of London, Newton was forced to isolation like many of us are during the pandemic. Away from everyone, and all alone for months on end, he decided to embrace the time to study, research and experiment. In doing so, this time period of waiting in the midst of crisis and all the pain that surrounded him and his community led Newton to come up with some of the most influential and groundbreaking discoveries in calculus and physics that changed the world. Perspective is an enormous factor when we face grave difficulty. How we respond to the challenges and trouble in our lives really defines who we are. I believe that there is a little bit of Newton in all of us. During these dark times and throughout the suffering, it is critical for us to rise up and tap into the spirit and fire that burns within us. Looking elsewhere will inevitably lead us to even greater heartache and despair. Hopefully we can find some glimmer of hope and have the resolve to keep fighting with the hopes that a breakthrough might be right on the other side of that next step. For in the midst of pain and suffering, there exists blessings. Look around you and open your eyes. There is good happening during our most trying times. A kind word, a smile, a card received in the mail, a text from a friend, a phone call, a prayer offered up for you or your family. These are small blessings that we may receive or give onto others that can be used as a springboard for us to rebound in our lives. My encouragement is to not overlook these blessings and to attach our hope onto them instead of other distractions that will take us far away from getting back on the path of life.

For centuries humans have looked to numerous things for answers to the pain that comes in and tried to rob them from living their best life. As people we naturally do not like suffering. Who does? The response and approach many of us take is to try to fill the void in our heart with something, anything that will take the discomfort away. Even having temporary relief is better than going through this daily affliction. Eventually, what we will come to realize is that nothing can fill the void. No thing can. It is unfortunate that so often people attempt to mask that pain with drugs, alcohol, money, and more possessions. You name it, people have tried it. No material goods, substance, or object will heal us or allow us to rebound. Only relationships can. Relationships are the essence of life, as we need human to human connection and support systems that can get us back to our truest selves. Family and friends are crucial, and yet still those people as amazing and influential as they are, alone, will not be completely enough.

We need a relationship with someone more powerful and more capable of transforming our lives than everyone we know and love combined. This one, the one who walked the earth and came for us all, this savior can truly set us free. I am talking about a relationship with Jesus. He is and provides in us that fire that burns within. Christ calls us daily because He loves us. Our brokenness, our sorrow, the good, the bad, and the ugly. To Him, it doesn't matter how we come to him, we can come freely as we are. Wounds and all. No matter what we have been through or what we face, no matter what we have done, he wants to help us carry that cross. Remember, he knows exactly what you face as He once carried that cross which weighed Him down. The Lord thirsts for our hearts and wants more than anything to see us filled with unexplainable joy that no one and nothing can take from us. Today, it is time to rebound, it is time for you to bounce back and take back the life that is yours!

Performing at the highest standard on the court takes a great amount of concentration, preparation, and of course practice. As any basketball player of a team knows, each member of the team is critical and plays a role in helping the unit achieve victory on the court. Five individuals must work together harmoniously and with great synchronicity to perform at a premier level. There are significant events, execution that must take place, and pieces to the puzzle that lead toward helping one's team win. Like my teammates, I worked exceptionally hard and was very fortunate to play Division II basketball for the Le Moyne College Dolphins in Syracuse, New York. My team, coached by Steve Evans and assisted by his dad, Stan "Buddy" Evans, along with Gallagher Driscoll, was composed of thirteen players over the three seasons I wore the green and gold. Even at the collegiate level, everyone has great ambition and a desire in wanting to be the star and score the basketball. There is something attractive to putting the ball in the basket and having your name called out over the PA system. We want to appear in the box score and every kid from the time they are old enough to play wants to keep track of their points per game. Scoring is where the glory is at, no doubt about it. Very rarely do you hear anyone talking about how many rebounds or assists or steals someone registered during a game. The common fan and within the inner circles of the basketball world, everyone mostly is super focused upon how many points you poured in for your team.

On my team, each player desired to win, but they also wanted to fill the stat sheet and be the "big man on campus." Yet, much of our team's success came not only from scoring the basketball, but from the bench players doing the intangibles and little things that add up. During competition in the NorthEast 10 Conference over my years as a college ball player, the victorious team who so often celebrated in the locker room after forty minutes of battling on the court, was often the one who had the most guys committed to doing the "dirty work." Moreover, when I look back it was the hustle plays, especially those willing to REBOUND the basketball, that lead us to win. Innumerable games where we eked out a victory by a matter of a few points before the final buzzer, was because of offensive and defensive rebounds. Getting another chance at a possession by grabbing a rebound after a missed shot or closing out one on defense with a board was crucial. It isn't talked about a ton outside of the locker room, but rebounding led us as a ball club at Le Moyne to many victories. Rebounds and second chance points were something we kept track of and highlighted when breaking down film after a game. Why, because it mattered!

Rebounds are huge on the hardwood at any level and they are essential in life. Although not the most glamorous, rebounding and winning the battle on the boards was by far one of the most pivotal parts to every game I played in. Life is very similar to the sport of basketball and rebounding. We miss shots constantly, as mistakes are made and we need to bounce back. Sometimes we make the same mistakes over and over and even when we are on top of our game, we miss an occasional shot and have to move forward to the next possession. Still, what about the times when the ball is not in our court so to speak and the air gets completely taken out of the ball? What about when we are deflated by life and a simple rebound is not going to save the game? How do we get back on track? I am talking about a loss. What do we do and how do we handle defeat? Quiet and nothing changes. Actually, if you throw in the towel you have to live with that defeat forever. Keep going and you provide another chance for yourself to overcome and be able to win in the end. What path will you take? It is easy to say the latter; however, saying and doing are too very different things. To dust yourself off, get back up, and have the courage to face it again is not easy. It takes great risk as we could fail again. Yet, there is that inner fire inside of us that pushes us to do so. When we respond to this drive inside and put all of our efforts and chips on the table, then we can know that we gave everything we had in striving for victory. No matter what the final scoreboard says, when you take this type of fierce approach towards life, you are a real winner!

It was November and the season was about to begin. We were boarding the team bus to take the short, ten mile trip from campus over to the Dome to play Syracuse. Before this trip over to SU, I had been in the iconic Carrier Dome numerous times as a kid growing up. I recall my dad taking me to my first Cuse game when I was seven years old. We made the three hour drive and I was so excited to enter the building I saw on ESPN during the big games. The enormous size of the top of the Dome can be seen from well over a mile away. I had my new Syracuse sweatshirt on and was thrilled to have a chance to watch my favorite players, at the time, take the floor for the Orange. Walking inside and seeing the court in person is something I will never forget. I couldn't believe I was in the Dome. Syracuse went on to win that day and I got to shoot a couple of baskets behind the bleachers at halftime where they sell all sorts of fan paraphernalia. I was in basketball Heaven! My dad even bought me a new Syracuse hat and a pin I put on it with Otto the Orange. I still have both to this day! Over the years my dad and I would go to games and sometimes my brother or grandpa would join us. It was always something I looked forward to. Sometimes I think back to my fifth grade journal entry in Ms. Race's class when I wrote about a Syracuse Orangemen game I went to during a school break. My mom saved the journal and showed me it before we played SU. In the paragraph I wrote about how my dream was to someday play on the Syracuse basketball team and win the championship for the Orange. Lofty goals as an elementary student, but that was my reality back then. When I got into the end of middle school and all throughout high school my parents sent me to Jim Boehim's basketball camp at Syracuse during the summers. This was huge for me as a rising star in the basketball world to go away and hoop it up against some of the kids who were invited to Five Star camps. I competed against some great ball players and had some amazing instruction from the coaching staff on the main court in the Dome!

At age 12, I was ready for Jim Boehim's basketball camp at Syracuse University.

Fast forward a number of years later and I was headed back to Syracuse to take on the Orange as a member of my college basketball team, the Le Moyne Dolphins. My team was abuzz with excitement to play on the big stage and have the opportunity to compete against one of the best D1 programs in the nation. Just walking out of the tunnel, after being in a state of the art locker room suiting up, was incredible. The setting was surreal, as I felt like I was in the pros with everything that was at our disposal from orange slices, to different kinds of energy drinks, Gatorades, warm towels, and other snacks. We could already hear the fanfare going on outside as we were ready to head out for warmups. This was not like our typical game day routine on campus or in any other gym that was practically the size of a shoe box in comparison to the monstrous Dome we were playing in today. Before getting up to say the pre game prayer, I took a moment to let it all sink in. I looked around at my teammates' faces who were excited for this chance to play on a very big stage. Coming this far for me personally was a huge deal. I was actually living out the dream I had all of those years ago. I was just wearing a different uniform.

As we exited the locker room and jogged out the tunnel, the band was playing in full force as we went through our lay-up lines and pregame routine. The fans were cheering and as I looked out into the student section, I could see a small contingency of people in the crowd dressed in Green and Gold amidst a sea of Orange. I relished every second of pregame warmups. I do so every game day, being a walk on, as court time was never a guarantee. However, today was an exceptional experience. Getting lots of shots up and sinking deep threes was extremely fun, but what I wanted most was to play and even more than anything to win! We stood on the foul line extended, arm and arm, for the National Anthem. Coach Evans went over the game plan with us one more time and called out the defensive assignments. As the ball was tossed in the air for the opening tip, I thought to myself, well this is it. I am here in uniform playing against my favorite team, Syraucse, let's see what happens. Over the first few minutes we worked through our nerves as a team and were going back and forth with the mighty Orange. It is always interesting to play against four or five guys on a single team that will be drafted into the NBA in a matter of months. Most people would be intimidated, but as an athlete and someone who works so hard every day, it is more respect than awe. When the ball is tossed in the air and the clock starts, everything else is set aside and it is time to battle. Suddenly, I looked up at the scoreboard and within a matter of a couple of minutes we were down by ten. The double digit lead for Syracuse grew rapidly to 20 points at the half. Walking into the locker room was a little tough because it sounded like a morgue. No one was talking and many heads were hung. I tried to get some of the guys to pick their heads up because we had to continue to compete. Midway through the second half we were down 30, 40...how could this be? Getting some minutes at the end of that game was a ton of fun for me personally, despite the score because I had always dreamt of this moment. Handling the ball out on the perimeter and blocking out hard for a rebound was unreal. I forgot how badly we were losing and got caught in the moment.

Playing Syracuse at the Dome was surreal for me, but losing to them by 50 was humiliating. Not the memory I was hoping for.

Walking off that court when the final horn rang was embarrassing. Our heads were hanging really low now as if we were being weighed down with a thousand pound boulder. My teammates looked like the walking dead. Syracuse had just obliterated us. As the sports saying goes, they took us behind the woodshed and destroyed us. We lost by 50! I will never forget that feeling. The feeling of defeat is one thing. This was one as an athlete that you take personally and it leaves the worst taste in your mouth. Welcome to the season. We had so much work to do. These types of losses and defeats in life often elicit a moment of truth. You can go one of two ways. You can give up and quit or you can find deep within you that fire that burns and wants it so bad that you will do whatever it takes to bounce back. I was not going to allow my team to be road kill and just waste a season away, we had work to do and the time to rebound was now.

Over the next week or so, we prepared, we trained, we practiced, and we competed harder than ever. We had to get ready for our first Division II opponent and the league games that were coming up in the near future. The coaching staff and players revved up their intensity in every area when we hit the court at our gym on campus. We even put in double practices, did extra small group work, and I stayed even later than normal with my fellow shooting guards to get another few hundred shots up. This was more than the usual four hundred or so jumpers we took daily. Why? Because it mattered. See when your why is big enough you will do anything to accomplish it. When you have a nasty taste in your mouth, when people are laughing at you when you walk off the court and you know you can be better, you use it as motivation. The loss can be turned into a fuel that energizes and inspires you to become even better, to become greater, to become stronger. That year we went on an incredible run. We went further than any team had done in years. Our basketball program soared to new heights as we won over 20 games and made it to the NorthEast 10 Conference Championship game. We battled and we fought. For forty minutes we laid it all out on the floor. Although we came up just short of winning the title, we had done our personal best. As a team we had done something that at the beginning of the season looked impossible. We had bounced back. We rebounded from a grave defeat and used it as a springboard to become the best team we could be.

The next season began. It was my senior year, the 2009-2010 campaign. The schedule was finally released and our first game would be against, who else, but Syracuse University. The mighty Orange who were pre-season ranked in the top 10, were favored by many to get back to the Final Four, and who would become the #1 team in the Nation along with a top seed in the NCAA Tournament for March Madness later that year. This was really our moment of truth. We had an opportunity to avenge our humiliating loss and to take some pride back. We had to perform better and compete for all forty minutes. We needed to do this for our team and for our college. When the team bus pulled up, we filed in for the quick ride over to the Dome. We all had a massive chip on our shoulders. The same locker room greated us, but it felt different this time. The fans heckled us during warm-ups louder than ever before and yelled some really obscene things. They told us we "did not belong on the floor" and pointed and laughed reminding us we had lost the previous year by 50 saying, "You are a joke." We were more prepared, well equipped, and had a different mindset. We went into that game believing we could get it done. I remember saying the prayer before the game that day, November 3rd, 2009. There was a different aura and divine spark that had been ignited. The fire was burning within us and we believed. I prayed for it, it was a matter of time to see if that big one would be answered and come true.

The first few minutes of the game were similar to the year prior. As the initial half was well under way, we were playing really well. Syracuse was probably thinking, why expound energy early on, we can just flip the switch and blow them out again. David versus Goliath, an insurmountable battle was at hand. By half time we were within four points and our morale was super high. The guys were high fiving each other and there was wind behind our sails. With about ten minutes to go in the second half, I looked up at the scoreboard. I thought to myself, we can really do this. With four minutes to go it was still a one possession game. Back and forth, shot for shot. There was no separation or run-away train this day. With less than a minute to go, during a time out our team was ultra focused. We realized the importance of this moment. We had a chance. We got a stop on defense and then called another time out. Coach drew up a play for our best shooter, Chris Johnson, an underclassman at the time. He rose to the occasion and with nine seconds as the clock wound down, he buried the biggest of his life and Le Moyne College basketball program history. All net! The Dome was silenced and we exploded in hysteria. The Orange faithful were shocked. Pandemonium broke out after Syracuse missed and the buzzer sounded. The final score read LeMoyne 82 vs. Syracuse 79. I jumped like Air Jordan, after his game winner to beat the Cavs, soaring high in the air and fist pumping! I had never felt a rush of enthusiasm and excitement as at that very moment. We had done it! The celebration began.

Any victory over the star studded Syracuse Orange team would have been sweet, but this one even sweeter because we bounced back in a historic manner. One could not have dreamt this scenario up any better! For that night we were truly the best team in Syracuse and held the keys to the city. No one could take away what we had accomplished. I remember waking up the next day after a long night of celebrating with my teammates and fellow college classmates, to turn on Sports Center. Scott Van Pelt was going through the top stories in sports and Le Moyne Basketball was it! I thought to myself that morning seeing our team on TV celebrating after the game, wow, that really just happened. Soaking in this historic moment is one that I will always remember and cherish. We took the world by storm that day and climbed Everest together! For me it was a most powerful example that anything is possible.

Our team celebrated with pure jubilation after the buzzer sounded & we took down Syracuse. I (far right) was elated to have been on the team that shocked the world.

When you work harder than ever before and bring out the best in each other, it is amazing to accomplish what people said couldn't be done. To be part of something greater than yourself and see collective efforts come to full fruition by bearing results that will remain forever, is exceptional! Rebounding and bouncing back. Being able to get back into the ring after being knocked out is not easy. Accepting the fact that you were not good enough and being humbled is hard. However, many lessons are learned in taking a loss. Losing can sometimes be our greatest teacher because it is during these moments that we really learn what we are made of. Greatness comes from within and having the heart of a champion doesn't mean keeping a perfect record. True champions are made in how they overcome defeat and use it to motivate them to become better than ever. And that is exactly what we had done.

As an athlete there is one thing that I dislike with a passion and that is losing. Losing is a hard pill to swallow no matter what. It is even more devastating when situations are out of our control and things like missed calls, lack of adjustment and poor decisions by the coaching staff are made, or cheating takes place. As the great John Wooden and legend of the game once said, "Success is peace of mind that is the direct result of self-satisfaction in knowing you did your best to become the best that you are capable of becoming." When we are fully prepared and give our very best effort in life and on the court, usually a positive result ensues. Sometimes, we can still face defeat, yet we do not have to hang our heads if we truly gave all we had and left nothing back. After winning ten national championships for the UCLA Bruins, and becoming the greatest coach of all time, John Wooden stepped down from the game of basketball. He was the greatest and yet he walked away. Some believe he had more to give.

Barry Sanders is yet another top athlete of all time. The Detroit Lions Hall of Fame running back had just rushed for over 2,000 yards and was less than one season away from breaking Walter Peyton's all time rushing record. Yet, he decided it was time and stepped away from the game. Unlike professional athletes or coaches, we cannot just step down and away from the game of life. Whether life is going well for us, but especially when it is not smooth sailing anymore or we face defeat, stepping down is not an option. There is no escape or "retirement" from life. So where can we go and who or what do we turn to when things start declining or even worse tailspin out of control at a moment's notice.

For many people that void and stress even on the surface level causes us to take part in things we normally would not do. We try to find an outlet in order to cope and deal with it; however, sometimes it is simply too much. We resort to increased eating, buying things we do not need, overconsumption of alcohol, gambling, drug use and other harmful behaviors. This is in an attempt to mask the pain. When we separate ourselves and can become detached from the issue we feel better. When we numb the discomfort and escape our reality for even just a little while, all seems well. No, actually it is worse. It is a lie. By trying to hide from the situation and escape it, we are again like the gazelle running from danger. We can run, but we certainly cannot hide. Eventually, we will run out of stamina and fall hard being snatched up by whatever obstacle life has thrown our way. The things human beings often seek are so transitory, here for a moment and gone before we know it.

There is no thing that can fill this void or erase the horrific pain we experience. No thing in this world will be able to truly allow us to move past, over, through, or around the negative situation, bad break or hardship. What we can do and must do is to attack the problem, face the issue, and deal with the situation. This is a daunting task. How can I get through the very thing that is causing me such agony and making my life flip upside down? Where will my strength come from in order to stop running from the pain like a gazelle which runs in fear and flip the script in order to start chasing down solutions that will lead me to devour life like a beast. How do I deal with those very challenges that continue to inhibit and disrupt my life? It comes from within. Deep down inside we have a spirit that is filled with abundant strength. There is a fire. Our Lord created us and gave us an advocate to come and to teach us all things and help us get through all the trials of life.

Over 2,000 years ago, centuries upon centuries before we were born, a man walked this earth with profound goodness and power that changed the game. He is my reason and He can be your reason as well. All you have to do is allow him in and Jesus will change your game forever. No matter what you are facing today, no matter how high the mountain is in front of you or how deep in the valley of despair you find yourself in, that is not the end of your story. Today, "I have set before you life and death, blessings and curses. Now choose life, so that you and your descendents might live." (Deuteronomy 30:19). It is a choice that we must make. I am not saying that it is easy or even simple. I do not know what you are going through or what you are facing as you read this book. What I do know for certain is that our God created us for life and He came so that we might have the most full life possible!

Today is the day for you to bounce back. Get up, dust yourself off and give it another shot. The greatest basketball player of all time Michael Jordan once said, "I have always believed that if you put in the work, the results will come." Now some things are out of our control, I know that very well and will share with you how this played a role in my life later on. Yet, as the saying goes...we can control what we can control and we must do our best to focus on our mindset. Let us start by focusing on one day at a time and winning the moment, the hour, the day. Let us not quit and may we continue to push forward. Quitting is NOT an option. God has something beautiful lined up for you and your future. There is something so big and so good on the other side of that Mountain. As the great football legend and coach Vince Lombardi is so famous for saying, "The man on top of the mountain didn't fall there." Tackle your problems, fight through adversity, overcome those challenges, defeat the enemy, and crush the negativity at all costs. When we do this and we allow God to aid us in our pursuit, we then become stronger, better, well equipped, more able, and a force to be reckoned with. It is then that we can and will win. When we have that approach and that hunger and drive we will be able to move forward and not look back. Living life this way is truly living and in the end our lives will be better than we could ever have imagined.

The road to victory is not an easy one. It is about doing the things that are not glamorous that lead one to win in the end. Rebounding the basketball is critical and rebounding in life when things go the wrong way is something we must do in order to succeed. Take these two hall of fame basketball players, Charles Barkley & Dennis Rodman. When people think about the greatest players of all time, you will not hear them mention Sir Charles or Hot-Rod who wore dresses to parties and dyed his hair the color of the rainbow. Nevertheless, those who know the game of basketball through and through and have a passion for being on the hardwood, like their teammates, understood that those exceptional athletes were crucial components for their team's success. What Charles and Dennis both did extraordinarily well was clean the glass, that is grab rebounds and attain the basketball. Playing with the likes of Michael Jordan and Julius Erving is a tall task. These guys scored the ball at an unbelievable clip; however, what every team needs in order to become great is a rebounder. That is where Dennis and Charles excelled. These guys didn't get the nicknames "The Worm" and "The Round Mound of Rebound" for nothing. They were dedicated, disciplined, and determined to get the ball back for their team so they could have another shot at scoring the ball in pursuit of victory.

Life is the same. You need to get the ball after life hits you hard and knocks you down. You and I must bounce back so we can get another shot at winning. You got this! Come with me on the journey and take the next step. Box out those negative thoughts, fight off that defeated mentality, and go after what you deserve. Attack that rebound, the ball won't just simply roll your way. You have to pursue it. You have to want it. Understand that the ball is now in your court. You can turn things around and even if it seems impossible to you, remember, nothing is impossible for God. As my best friend and wife likes to say after being amazed by the Lord working in her life, "Won't He do it!" He will do it and we can get through it. Believe that things will get better, but like any good comeback it can take a little time and will require some real effort. Easy roads lead to dead ends. The path of victory is hard, but well worth it. Set your mind on what you desire and make it happen. It is time to bounce back and rebound.

CHALLENGE #2: How can you rebound & bounce back?

The second challenge is for you to examine where you could bounce back or rebound in your life. Think about something that has caused you a great deal of heartache or stress lately. What situation, event, or maybe relationship needs to be moved on from. How can you get back on top? Write down the thing that has caused you distress and then jot down some ways you will actively bounce back from it.

"In order to win in life, you have to stop sitting on the sidelines & enter the game. Life is not a spectator sport nor is it a cake walk. Trials will come your way. You will be tested, but if you remain determined, victory will be yours." -Dan Jason (Author)

CHAPTER 4: Entering the Game

How it starts doesn't determine your destiny. On October 20, 1988 I was born into a loving home of two parents, Rick & Carol Ann, who were grounded in good morals and faith. My parents were hard working teachers who loved my brother, Brandan, and I and did everything possible to provide for our family. They saved, sacrificed, and did anything within their power to give us a happy life. We did not desire much as kids and there was always a home cooked meal on the table for dinner each evening. My favorite was my mom's homemade sauce, ziti, and meatballs with a side of garlic bread of course. I can smell that aroma from a mile away. You can call me what you want, just don't call me late for dinner, especially that Italian feast! I can say that we always went on family vacations each summer and eventually we would travel to some really exotic destinations. I mean who at the age of 14 had been to Hawaii twice and a number of different countries that as a kid I could barely pronounce the names of. I was blessed. Sunday dinner at Nanny and Grandpa's house on the Hill was a family staple. All my cousins, aunts and uncles would gather for summer cookouts as Gramp fired up the Barbeque or we would indulge in some comfort food during the cold winter months. As a young man, growing up in Germantown, New York, my life would be perceived by most as having been "perfect."

I was a child of two highly educated and loving parents, who valued education. Being raised in a white middle class family that took me around the world and back again was exceptional. I was constantly supported, loved, and taught important life lessons on how to be a better person and why giving back mattered. My little brother, Brandan, adored me. He was my best friend and practically worshipped the ground I walked on. If I got the latest Air Jordans, you better believe that little bro was rocking the same fresh kicks along with me. If Dan was strutting around in a new pair of jeans and top of the line Nike windbreaker jacket, my little brother was twining along with me. He was my shadow and a great one at that. My ride or die and my homeboy. I could not have had a closer friend then all those years ago as a kid or now than my sidekick and younger brother.

I also was fortunate to have grown up on the family compound. We call it *The Hill*. It is a large piece of property which my great grandfather, Carmine, had bought almost a century ago after coming over from Italy. *The Hill* is the first and only childhood home I would know and is where I still go back to today to see my people-my family. As a kid I was practically smothered by my grandparents, aunts, uncles, and cousins who were always around. You couldn't escape them even if you wanted to. Proximity is a real thing and we could hit each other's houses with a baseball. Funny thing is during spring and summer time, our games of homerun derby made that a fairly consistent reality. Sorry mom and Nanny for those broken lawn ornaments and occasionally smashed in windows. My "perfect" family on *The Hill* supported me and everyone was involved in my life in a positive manner. The people in my family, those in my corner were the best a kid could possibly have. Love was abundant and I did not have a care in the world. But as we all know so well, there is no actual "perfect" and life has a way to become interesting to say the least as you get older.

Growing up on *The HILL* there were always Sunday dinners at Nan and Gramp's house and lots of time with the cousins.

On Waikiki Beach in Hawaii on a summer family vacation.

After a fantastic childhood filled with amazing birthday parties, holidays, sit down dinners as a family each night, and tons of engagement in sports, I entered my teenage years. This twelve year old kid was turning thirteen and this joyful boy who had not a negative bone in his body, would soon face a wave of darkness that is unexplainable and incomprehensible. Before we get into what transpired, what would change the game for me from winning in life to losing, and what sent me tailspinning out of control like a helicopter caught in a hurricane, let's take a moment to discuss some things.

Adolescence is typically a hard transition for kids going from one state in life to another. Yet, the challenge of growing up is not what we are talking about here with regard to my situation. As I mentioned before, I was part of a family of four, raised on good morals and values. We went to Catholic mass every Sunday growing up and my faith really began to expand by the time I was ten or so. I recall sitting in Church one Sunday morning in mid October when the vocations director, Jim Walsh, came down from Albany and spoke to our parish. Sitting in the eighth pew in the Church of the Nativity in Linlithgo, I heard words that seemed to strike me like a lightning bolt. Father Walsh was discussing young men being called to the priesthood and said, "We need faith filled young men to become priests and lead the Church." I felt like he was speaking directly to me. Not only did I listen intently, I felt the Holy Spirit jump in me and my heart and soul tingle with sensation. It was from that moment on that I listened to the Lord and his calling on my life...I would become a Catholic Priest.

What else could a person possibly do to contribute more to society and to God's Kingdom than to become a priest and administer the sacraments. After all, we are called to be saints and to be holy. We are called to lead others as the Lord's disciples and the priest is the shepherd of the Church. A "Father" of a parish is responsible for bringing souls to Jesus Christ. Even as a young child I began reading the bible on my own and praying daily, delving into the word and communicating with God multiple times throughout the day. Not a day went by that I did not pray or think about the Lord or feel Him calling me to spend time with Him and His Son. Routinely, I woke up ready for a great day ahead and thanked God for the new day. I said some morning prayers and then prayed before I ate. I then went to school and like a normal kid, I played sports. I remained God centered and focused and I always prayed before my meals and before my games. I even prayed to do well on my assignments and thanked the Lord for his goodness throughout the day.

During the summer, before I went into 7th grade, I spent a ton of time reading the bible and getting into understanding scripture. I went to early morning mass on the weekends with my dad since I was about two years old and always desired to be on the altar. I went from going up to the lectern with my dad as a toddler to altar server the day after making my First Holy Communion. Soon thereafter, I became a lead altar server by the 4th grade. If I could live at church at this point and time in my life I would have. It was a sanctuary, the place as a child and as a pre-teen that I desired to be. I understand that this is not necessarily normal for someone so young, but at the time it was just my life and what I did. The feeling and desire was normal to me and for me. During the mass I felt a calming sense of peace and I could truly sense God's presence. Most of all I was able to receive the Eucharist, which I always believed was truly the body and blood of Christ.

As a second grader, I was thrilled to make my Holy Communion and was excited to bring up the gifts.

While growing up, my dad always taught me to give my best and to put forth my all in whatever I did. He said that no matter what would happen in life, I would be able to sleep well at night knowing I gave my best effort and this was what mattered most. My mom was the nicest and most sweet person I could have ever learned from and she taught me to respect everyone including, myself. There might not have been a more "All American Family" or a better childhood. I say this not to boast, but to articulate a point. Things were fantastic, as good as they could be. Until...Well, then things went down-hill unexpectedly and the light grew dark really really fast. Pain and defeat was on its way.

How are you, they would ask? "I'm fine" or "I'm good." That was the biggest load of steamy bull carp that anyone had ever uttered. I wish I were. And that is one of the major problems we face today. People have this desire to pretend that everything is always okay. "I'm fine," is probably one of the most common responses and you are lying through your teeth. No, we are not fine and things aren't always okay. For me it was anything but good and I was trying to escape the question people wanted to ask before they even answered it. Parents, grandparents, family members, teachers, friends, acquaintances, they all ask how you are doing. Did they really want to know. Do they really ever want to truly know? I wonder this now about people and thinking about my life as a teen, no one really wanted to know because if they did they would have been entering a nightmare with me. Oh and I am not simply referring to being shoved into lockers on a daily basis, having plastic bags put over my head as kids tried to suffocate me on the back of the school bus, or people spitting in my hair thinking it was funny. This is not about gossip or note passing, I am not talking about having to eat by yourself on an island in the lunchroom because you are a nerd or a "goody two shoes." The physical and psychological bullying that I endured was grave enough. I'm talking about a violent storm coming through and striking with Tornado like force, flipping your life completely upside down and throwing you into the next galaxy. I had no idea what was on its way, but it was coming!

After turning 13 and realizing I now had to shave some stubble, take care of these annoying pimples, and grow into my lanky body, life didn't seem so different. I had always had a unique faith, although my friends and peers as I grew older did not care too much for that side of things. The group I would hang out with at school, play sports with on the GCS teams, and those I competed with in the town leagues were typical teenagers. They were solely into their friends, consumed by video games, and began testing the waters with life. Some of them became interested in drinking and drugs, while others began committing some petty crimes. This stuff was all definitely not what I wanted to associate with or be about. I went from having a lot of friends during childhood, to numerous peers who I enjoyed being around to hardly no one in my corner. All things considered, things were still fairly well because I had my best friend in my brother and my cousin who I now did everything with. We went to school, came home, did our homework and then rushed outside to play ball on the blacktop until sundown. Sometimes we even went back out on the court after dark, putting on the flood light to play until our moms had to yell at us to come in for a shower before hitting bed.

See in life whether it begins extremely well like mine did or if it started out as a disaster, your destiny is not determined. You have what it takes to play the hand based on the cards you are dealt. Some of you reading this are thinking right now, wow, that sounds a lot like my childhood. While, others had quite the opposite experience. No matter what your starting spot was or what your initial lot was in life, all of it is truly luck of the draw. The start really boils down to fate or chance. However you want to say or slice it, the way it started is not going to be the way it ends, nor does it have to or should it control your trajectory in life.

Smooth sailing will only last for a while, the boat that goes out to sea will eventually run into a raging storm. Boats were not meant to stay at harbor, but to sail. Storms and great floods can infiltrate our lives and rock our boat—shake our world. Then, in these moments, what do we do? Do we sit there and take on the water and sink? Or do we adjust to the situation and start bailing the water out. God will bail us out when we go through the storm. Nonetheless, if we forget to ask for help or do not believe it will get better, then it won't. For He has promised us that if we "ask and it will be given to you, seek and you will find. Knock and the door will be opened. For everyone who asks, receives. He who seeks, finds, and the one who knocks, the door is opened." (Matthew 7:7). Is it that easy and simple all the time? All we really have to do is just to ask? No it is not that easy. I know and you are probably sitting there thinking I have asked for numerous things and many times for God to take away what was causing me the suffering, yet it continued. Well, sometimes we are asking and we must wait. After all, Jesus cried out to God for help first in the garden before he faced his passion and death. He painfully pleaded with God saying, "Father let this cup pass from me, not my will but yours be done." A number of hours later the Lord who cried out to God again with great anxt shouting, "Eloi, Eloi, Lema Sabachthani, My God, My God, Why have you abandoned me?"

Have you ever felt abandoned by God or cried out for help in desperation? I have, and if you experienced this or know someone who has it is a great plea for help because hope was gone. It evaporated and was not even in our realm of possibility. Faith is essential for hope to exist and hope is certainly vital for one to believe in a future filled with goodness. As the Word says, "Hope deferred makes the heart sick," and "faith is the substance of things hoped for and the evidence of things not yet seen." (Proverbs 13:12, Hebrews 11:1). When we have faith then we can have hope and when we have hope, then we tend to have increased measures of faith. Interestingly enough, faith and hope, they go hand in hand. It is during the most trying times of our lives that we need to latch onto God the most and tap into our faith. Even when we cannot feel His presence, it is in these moments that we must remember that a flame does still exist in our heart, even if it is just a mere ember. If we will do this and stand firm, then we will receive an increased measure of faith and the trials we face will not only make us stronger, but will mark us with the crown of life that God promises to those who love Him. The game of life is not easy and cannot be won without effort. We never know when the tides will turn, but we must be on our guard for the enemy and evil are seeking to steal what we have, and turn us away from and against God.

"The darkness that was within me was all consuming. I was trapped in a pit of horrid despair so deep I knew my life would soon be ending. It was time to surrender."

-Author, Dan Jason

CHAPTER 5: Dancing with the Devil

"The devil fears hearts on Fire with love of God."
-Saint Catherine of Siena

The funny little guy dressed in red, with horns and a pointy tail. Shall we dance? It was a cold dark and dreary day. I was home alone after school and quietly working on my homework. This was par for the course before heading to practice. I looked over my shoulder and I thought perhaps my brother was home and didn't know that I had just entered our house. "Bran," I called. I went upstairs and checked his room. He wasn't in there. I looked in my room. Nowhere to be found. Huh, that was weird. Okay, well back to work on that advanced algebra and world history homework which was due tomorrow. Then it happened again. Someone or something was looking at me. I could feel it. There was a presence in my house and I got up quickly and ran outside. I decided to sprint up to my grandparents house for an impromptu visit. Milk and cookies with Nan would certainly calm my nerves. After seeing my mom's car go down the long driveway and pull into the garage, I said to Nan, "I got to go. Mom's home and I don't want to be late for practice." I walked into my house and my mom asked where I had been. I told her, "Just visiting Nanny and Grandpa." "Well that is nice of you, you are such a caring young man. Don't let that ever leave you, they always love your company." I was freaked out. What the heck just happened a mere hour ago? What was going on and what was I going to do. The next day I came home from school and entered into my routine not thinking anything of it. This time I was in my room changing and someone was looking at me, staring at me. That same creepy and eerie feeling came over me. I ran downstairs and turned the TV on to distract my attention, maybe the noise would make it go away...There was undoubtedly a presence in my house and it was not Casper the friendly ghost. The dance would continue and evil would not be doing a beautiful ballet...

By definition, light is visually perceived radiant energy that is just a small segment of the electromagnetic spectrum. Light is a property and quality that human beings and all creatures for that matter need and are constantly attracted to. We desire to be in the light and to be surrounded by bright things. Out of necessity we must have light in order to see. Light is quintessential for us on our planet to be able to function, and to know what is before us. The physics of light according to Google involves the following, "light sometimes refers to electromagnetic radiation of any wavelength, whether visible or not. In this sense, gamma rays, X-rays, microwaves and radio waves are also light." So what does that all mean for us when we unpack it and break it down to a more basic human level for functionality. Basically, we need this substance to survive and without it, like a plant that has to have energy from the Sun, we would not stay alive, let alone be able to thrive.

Furthermore, light and radiant energy that stems from light is desired by humans and creation for other reasons oustive of survival. People are more positively influenced by those who wear a bright smile and have an upbeat and energetic mood. Lightheartedness comes from those positive vibes and the glimpse of light that is shared. After all, Jesus calls us the "children of the light." We were created in this way and are meant to be part of this positive life force and energy system of shining brightly and giving off a glow. This luminescens we radiate internally so to speak, transmits a tangible force that is emitted to those who we encounter in an external fashion.

According to Webster's Dictionary, Darkness is the partial or total absence of light. Darkness is not desired and is something many people are naturally afraid of. This is because whether we know it or not, we were created in God's image and likeness and filled with light from the start. The scriptures clearly lay this out to us by saying, "For you are all children of light, children of the day. We are not of the night or of the darkness." (1 Thessalonians 5:5) No one wants to be surrounded by darkness, doom or despair. It is not in our DNA, nor will it ever be, to be engulfed by nightfall. Still, life does not discriminate. It certainly would not be our personal choice to have to go up against dark times, but there are many people who face this darkness today and others who will have to battle it in the future inevitably. For us when we do go toe to toe with this black hole and emptiness in our lives, we may never know why it came about in the first place. Some people bring darkness into their own life by making erratic decisions or horrible choices. When this is the case, we at least have a reason for the situation that is being faced. While others are victims of horrific events and circumstances that they never would wish on their worst enemy. The darkness that chases them down is no fault of their own and was totally out of their control.

What I am about to share with you in this next section is not for the faint of heart. For a while I debated how much to share and in what capacity. Nevertheless, I decided to hold nothing back. This is not hyperbole or written for dramatic effect. I am not talking about some pansy ass bullshit box office hit like *Nightmare on Elm Street* or *Freddy & Jason*. Pardon my french. There was a time in my life when I actually danced with the Devil. I engaged in a war with evil that is unlike any nightmare I could have imagined. Everything I share actually happened and is thankfully a thing of the distant past. The reason why I am revealing the darkest days in my own life is to explain, show, and emphasize that no matter what we face we can overcome it. The other reason is to highlight that evil does exist in our world and causes a ton of problems and heartache. We can overcome this evil and the power of darkness, but in order to do so we must have the light and powerful fire burning within us. On our own, it is impossible.

Jim Valvano led his NC State Wolfpack team to an improbable NCAA basketball national championship against the heavily favored and mighty Houston Cougars in 1983. The historic championship run led by Jim, the head coach, and man of great inspiration is a reminder that David does slay Goliath and as bleak as the prognosis looks, faith and playing the game will determine the final score. Valvano said so emphatically in his ESPY speech when he was dying from cancer, "Don't give up. Don't ever give up." I hope that you come to realize that there is nothing too great and no darkness too strong that God is incapable of carrying us through. Not only will He carry us through it and make a way when we cannot find a way, but we will more than survive. God has the ability to take something so bad and so evil and turn it into something good later on. It is critical that we understand that God does not desire evil or the darkness that infiltrates our lives; however, through His power and grace He carries us through it all and turns our life around for the good. This is what He did for me and I believe that He can and will do for you during your times of greatest despair.

I am grateful to say that I was surrounded by light and was spiritually and emotionally shining for most of my life, until my 15th birthday. It was then that the darkness engulfed me like a Tsunami ready to destroy and wash away my very being. All these years later, I often wonder why. So many of us wonder why bad things happen to good people. We may never know. As for me, darkness did not just creep into my life, it submerged me and became the essence of my life. It was as if someone went over to the wall and flipped the switch from "on" to "off," or turned the faucet from "hot" to "cold." In a matter of a second, in an instant, the room goes from bright and vivacious to pitch black and an eerie stillness that is extremely uninviting. Light changes to darkness fairly quickly with the setting of the sun each day. Yet, there is still a process and the half hour or so gives us time to adjust. Lamentably, my life changed instantaneously and I did not know if it would ever change back.

As I struggled through my sophomore year in high school, little by little my world grew increasingly darker and darker. It went from light to dark, bam, like that. But the darkness became thicker and deeper. My world grew colder and scarier day by day. The light and energy was sucked out of me, as my mentality changed and I began to view the world in a cynical and negative manner. The happy kid who loved sports and was thrilled to be part of such a loving family, started to become a shell of himself. I could feel a total change take place. It was as clear as changing your underwear or putting on a different pair of shoes. It was tangible and I hated it. Dramatic differences were noticed when I woke up in the morning and didn't want to get out of bed and tackle the day. I was not the same happy go lucky kid who loved playing with his brother or could shoot baskets with his cousin after school for hours anymore. Something was wrong. It is one thing to have to get out your umbrella when the rain starts to come down from the sky, it is a whole other story when the floodgates open and the levee breaks and you have no shelter. During these times when you are doing everything and anything possible to simply stay alive, while being tossed around like a rag doll in the middle of a storm surge that has no end in sight, it is time to sink or swim. For me I was sinking and sinking fast...what was my life coming to? The dance continued and I had no other choice but to submit to the evil puppet pulling the strings.

At first I did not know what was fully going on. I could feel it, but it didn't register and it was something that seemed just off. But then as time marched on and this darkness grew and clamped down on me, it was evident that I was being attacked. A dark cloud was like a shadow standing over me that I could not shake. What really freaked me out was that I could feel a horribly evil presence continuously creeping in and it was not just my imagination. I began to spiral out of control and into a horrid depression. The worst was being alone. The threads of any relationships I still had at school or in my own family were being unspooled and were unraveling quicker than ever. The very people who were nice enough to befriend me, the loser, vanished as I went down the tubes and I kept only to myself. I began to see everything I did as evil and wrong and the darkness clenched my soul and took a hold of me. It was not just a darkness or depression, it was more.

Many people will live their entire life without thinking about darkness to the level I experienced. For this I am grateful because no one should have to even imagine what I went through, let alone have to consider how to endure it for even a short period of time in their life. Sure, all of us go through hard times, that is part of life. We will all face the loss of a loved one someday. We have to deal with disappointing events, some tragic news, disease that strikes in the form of cancer or even some other form of despair. Nonetheless, not many people think about evil on the level that I faced. Most will never even know that it exists or is such a powerful force. For this too I am thankful. The darkness that I walked through was sheer terror, some people might have faced a moment of this in their lifetime, but I was forced to dance with the Devil. Yeah, that is right, I said it. The Devil. He is real and prowling around seeking to devour souls. St. Michael the Archangel is needed now, more than ever before to protect us against this wickedness. Jesus warned us of this evil when He said, "The thief (Satan) only comes to steal, kill, and destroy, but I have come to give them life and to give it more abundantly" (John 10:10) Evil is real. Satan filled my heart with darkness and took away all the light that used to be inside of me. The Devil impacted me and then sent demons to torment me in an attempt to make me give up and quit on God, not to mention to quit on myself.

Every seemingly positive thought I used to have was now pure darkness. I always prided myself on respecting others, being nonjudgmental, having a willingness to listen, and of course offering a helping hand. This was because that was after all, the right thing to do. When I spoke to people during this dark time in my life, I cursed them out in my mind. I would diss them to extreme levels. And the most horrible and evil thoughts one could ever imagine filled my brain. I hated them. Well, a distinction must be made, I did not hate those people, but the evil one living inside of me, he did. So, this led me to always want to be alone. I desired isolation. This was not my natural tendency. I had always been a kid who loved being around others, but now I did not because I could not handle the agony and did not want to drag down anyone else while I suffered this living hell.

Isolation is a bad bad thing. Darkness storms in when we are isolated because we have nowhere to go and we cannot hide. Why would anyone want to be isolated when they were going through such agonizing times? Let me re-emphasize something important here. It wasn't that I really wanted to be isolated, it was that Satan tricked me into thinking that I didn't deserve to be with anyone and that it was better for me to be alone than to sin gravely against them. It was the thought that being alone was less damaging to others than to be with them and to be cursing people out in my mind and disrespecting them to no end. No man is an island and no man should be alone. God did not make man to be in isolation. In fact, He made man, namely Adam and created the animals and earth for the man. Yet, all of these good things that God created did not appease the man, as none were a suitable partner for Him. Therefore, God created a woman, her name was Eve. When this occurred, at last then the man was content. God said after this process of creating the woman, that It was very good. She was very good indeed. This points to the fact that humans are therefore relational and it is the very desire of the person to be one with others in the community. We want to be liked, we have a craving for this positive attention, and we want to have an exchange of love. This longing for belonging and love needs to take some shape and allows us to remain connected albeit family, clan, tribe, gang, church, group, or team.

Not me! I ended up locking myself in my room for hours on end. I was an island and no one was allowed in. No one could come or wanted to come to visit me. I was all alone, just where the Devil wanted me. Even Jesus wasn't allowed in. This was the biggest problem of all. The very Lord who I loved so much even as a child, the one who gave me life, light, purpose, and meaning was shut out. He who I dedicated my life to at age 11 and decided I would serve as a faithful priest for the rest of my life…He was locked out and not let in. What is even worse is that Jesus was cursed at, belittled, mocked, and humiliated by me with every thought that came to my mind when I looked at the crucifix. All I could think about was "why are you crucifying me?" The thoughts continued to swirl in my mind… "Why did you, Daniel, drive the nails in my hands and spikes into my feet?" I didn't think of them anymore, they came and I couldn't control them. And then there were voices…I had to turn and trust in the Lord during this dark point, but how? Psalm 23:1-4 says the following:

The LORD is my shepherd; there is nothing I shall want

In green pastures he makes me lie down; to still waters he leads me;

He restores my soul. He guides me along the right paths for the sake of his name.

Even though I walk through the valley of the shadow of death,

I will fear no evil, for you are with me; your rod and your staff comfort me.

When demons come upon you and overtake you they infest your brain and attack your soul. The voices that I heard in my head were pure evil. These were not my own thoughts, they were the Devil and his companions trying to destroy me. I heard different variations of voices in my head and around me. They grew louder and louder. The worst was at night time. I dreaded the setting of the sun. What should be such a beautiful occasion and colorful painting in the sky was a bismal indication as the clock struck an hour that it was night again for me. I hated the night. Darkness was the Devil's playground when I was in high school. Nothing was worse for me than being alone at night. The noises I heard in my house, the presence I felt lurking in the darkness...I cannot fully explain in words the sheer terror I faced and still the worst was to come...It was time to go to bed. Countless nights I would hide under my covers trying to escape the voices, the presence that loomed in my room and around me. Then, as if it could not get any worse, it did. I physically shook in terror and my heart sank deep within me as my bed shook and screaming was racing through my mind. I thought I was going to die. Night after night I was sweating and lived the full nightmare which was my dark reality. One night what transpired was a scene right from the movie The Exorcist. I felt my very soul leave my body and I saw a bright white light. My life was over. I shot up so fast as if I was launched up an elevator shaft and was blinded by the brightest light. And then the light went out, pitch black darkness. My soul sank back into my body and I knew that I was still alive. How this happened or what took place is still a mystery to me. It was as if the Evil one tried to take my soul, but Jesus would not allow him to destroy me and my life was spared.

One small issue I faced during the day to day turned into a monumental struggle that captured me like a ship being tossed to and fro amidst the rainy sea. I started hearing all kinds of voices in my head during the daytime too and I began to be tormented at every hour and every second of the day.. The Devil was speaking lies to me and I was listening.

I heard all sorts of lies that started out as small things such as, "You are worthless," and "No one loves you," or "You are no good, you are evil." I knew these weren't true or were they? When you hear this negativity inside of yourself for countless days on end and you can't shut out the voices in your head, you begin to believe them. I began hearing and believing all of these things. I thought to myself, *wow no one cares and I am not loved, maybe you don't deserve to live anymore... just end it all.*

By age 16 my depression had spiraled immensely and I was on average trying to pray away my problems for hours a day asking God's constant forgiveness and obsessively making the signs of the cross in public and in private. The voices in my head now more numerous than ever continued and wouldn't cease. Did I have to be alone again, would this ever end. Oh no, the sun was going down, it was night again. I heard the evil presence walking behind me as I ran to my room. I was scared. I was terrified. I was exhausted and I wanted to die. The Devil had sent demons that were relentless and now I began hurting myself. My inner pain turned into external outer pain manifesting itself in self torture.

It started with pinching and small scratching. Then it turned into punching myself in the legs and arms and even head. I began cutting my arms with my finger nails. Why? The voices were not stopping and now I was cursing out my family, the ones who loved me the most. I was cursing out God and even Jesus when I looked at the cross. I found myself yelling daily, in an uncontrollable manner. I was a volcano that had so much pressure on the inside that had built up and I was ready to explode at any moment. The Devil knew I was alone and he still wanted my soul and wasn't giving up.

By age 17 during my senior year I was locking myself daily in the bathroom at school or at home for countless minutes because I could not handle the voices in my head or looking at people and hearing the demons say sickening things. The evil spirits were taking over and I did not know what to do. I could not allow others to see me constantly cutting myself or inflicting wounds. I screamed because my heart was empty and in so much agony. If life were to go on like this I did not know how I could endure. I did not want to live anymore and felt it would be pleasant to die. At night I kept waking up due to tremors and horrific nightmares. And then once again it was a really bad night. The bed began shaking like so often it would, but this time I heard demons speaking out loud to me and saw their evil little auras on the end of my bed. I started screaming bloody murder out loud in the night and my parents came rushing into my room.

Shortly thereafter I made up my mind, I had no other choice. I got home from school on April 14, 2006 in the afternoon around 3:30pm and closed my door. I was alone, well besides the Devil who was always waiting for me ready to dance. Sure, my parents and brother would probably be home soon, but what did it matter. Inevitably, they would find me, but I had to end this dance once and for all. I could not keep going like this any longer nor did I have any desire or fight left in me. My soul was a bloody mess. I was a boxer against the ropes with the clock running down and I fell. Against the mat the ref was counting to signify the knockout punch. Another second or two and it would be over. Should I write a note? There was no point because what good would that do. No one would understand no matter what I jotted down on a mere piece of paper. So it was time. The hour had come. The curtain was about to fall on me, the 17 year old teen and I was more ready than ever to ring the bell and give up the fight. Sad yes, but true. I could not imagine hell was worse than what I now faced 24 hours a day so I would take the chance and live with what happened when my soul left this world.

I was ready to committ suicide. Killing myself was my only escape from the darkness.

I remember vividly the scene so many years later, as it plays out like a movie in my mind. I opened my closet door and grabbed the belt. I put it on a very solid hook that was attached to a wooden rod in my closet. I felt the leather around my hands and knew it would do the job. I was certain it would work and the misery would end. Suffocating to death would be a fairly quick and less gruesome way to die. At least then, whoever found me would not be faced with a bloody mess. At that very moment, now having been in my room for a number of hours, the sun was starting to wane. I heard a voice. It was a much different voice than the evil spirits and demons that had ransacked my life and tormented me for the past few years. It was the voice of God. Just before I could tighten that cold leather belt around my neck, I dropped to my knees when I heard God speak to me. As clear and loud as day He said boldly, "Your life is not over. Don't do it." I wept like a baby uncontrollably for the next what seemed like hours. God had saved my life. I literally had been to the moment of my last breath and had been spared, the first miracle is often the greatest. I did not commit suicide that day, but instead I asked God to help me. I prayed that the Devil and evil spirits would leave me forever and that my life would be given back to me.

A few days later I went and visited our parish priest, Father Gerken. I told him about the evil spirits and demons. I told him that I believed that I was possessed by the Devil. He believed me when I recalled what I was going through and so he performed anointing of the sick and said prayers to cast out the demons. I felt as if a war was going on inside of me! And then he blessed me with the holy chrism oil. When Father Gerken made the sign of the cross on my forehead with the oil and prayed over me I felt different.

The next few days I did not hear voices anymore and the evil thoughts began to go away. Within a number of months it was as if my "house had been swept clean." In the past the horrific voices, the evil mentality, the rage and anger had controlled my life. Now it was no longer there, although I was afraid it might return. The dark presence was also gone and it wasn't just out for the night, God must have posted a no vacancy sign because it wouldn't return.

During these three dark years of my life there was just one moment that I had perfect peace in and pure joy filled my heart. Every time I was at mass and the priest consecrated the host I had peace. At the very pinnacle of the consecration prayer as the priest held it up the Blessed Sacrament and when I received Christ in the Eucharist, I was able to escape. All of the evil and the torment subsided for a brief moment. Sometimes the peace lasted for five seconds and other times a minute. I knew at that instant during the mass, that Jesus Christ was truly present in the Eucharist and that He was going to turn my life around. The power of the Son of God can transform anyone and bring us back into the light. When you are in a dark spot recall the power of these words, "I am the light of the world, whoever follows me will not walk in darkness, but will have the light of life." (John 8:12)

"There is a reason why the rearview mirror is much smaller than the windshield. It is because the things of the past are behind us and we must keep our eyes focused on what is in front of us and on our future."

-Joel Osteen

CHAPTER 6: Glimmer of Light

"I took my troubles to the LORD; I cried out to him,
and he answered my prayer." (Psalm 120:1)

When I graduated high school from Germantown Central in late June of 2006, I headed off to Le Moyne College, a small Jesuit school in central New York to study religious studies and theology. I was set on and excited to prepare to become a Catholic Priest. I knew that this was what I needed to do, after all, God literally saved my life. Little did I know that as I write this now at 31 years old, I would be happily married to the love of my life, have hope of children of my own someday, and be working for NOVUS, a custom apparel company with some of my most faith filled friends. Little did I know that I would have taught for eight years in the inner city, have become a lector and Eucharistic minister at one of the most vibrant parishes in Albany, grow and lead a young adult faith group, develop a ministry in serving the homeless at the Capital City Rescue Mission, and serve on multiple boards for our Church. In addition, my passion has come fully alive in the beautiful opportunities I have had in entering the jails to become a prison ministry team leader at Greene Correctional Facility in Coxsackie, NY as well as serving the poor on the streets and in the dump of Mexico City, as well as those suffering on the Native American Reservations in the midwest U.S.

God has a sense of humor I guess. If I would have known all of this, let alone the miracles that I have witnessed over the past decade, I might have been overwhelmed. What I do know is that you can rebound and when you have Christ as a central part of your inner circle, He will help you find the way..."I am the way, the truth, and the life. No one comes to the Father except through me." (John 14:6).

If you are in a dark spot, keep battling and know that you can and will rebound. Trust in God and He will help you bounce back.

Your time is coming and the light is about to break through amidst all of the darkness. Do not give up or give in to the dark side. The lies and the deceit might seem endless. The depression and anxiety or pain and suffering might be weighing you down, but your destiny has not been fulfilled. Jesus will help you carry your cross and your resurrection Sunday is coming. See, I was experiencing what seemed like an eternal **FRIDAY** in my life. I felt as if I was going to carry that cross forever and my life was truly a living Hell. But now, I am free of the chains, free of the vice grip of hatred and evil. For Christ has set me free and I have that fire burning within me once again, as "The light keeps shining in the dark, and darkness has never put it out." (John 1:5)

    I celebrated with my family after graduating from Germantown High School. I was excited for a new beginning and fresh start at Le Moyne College! That would be where my life turned around.

We do not walk this road alone and there are people praying for you right now. If you are reading this book it is for a reason. You did not get a hold of it by chance or some sort of randomness. It is because there was something that you needed to know, a message that could put a new song in your heart. God wants to see the light shine in you again. Your life has purpose and it has meaning. There is only one you in this world and there will only be one you for all eternity. Think about that for a moment and let it settle in. Nobody else in the history of creation can replicate you and all of the things you have to offer this world during your one precious lifetime. Despite what you have gone through and all that you continue to battle, keep in mind, "No weapon formed against me shall prosper." (Isaiah 54:7). You have what it takes, dig deep, and believe. Grab that rebound, claim for yourself that fresh start and new beginning today. Know and believe in your heart that the next shot you take will go in. If you give up now, if you raise the flag of surrender, the beauty of your life and your story will not be told. Be bold and carry on, for you are a warrior. Regain your enthusiasm and zeal for life and allow this be your motto, "We can and we will do hard things!"

The following words by St. Paul have become a type of anthem for my renewed life. I can relate so much to him because of where he came from and how God completely turned his life around. When Paul came to the realization that his life had so much more meaning and importance, the fire was stoked again. His strength, vigor, and energy were harnessed in a positive direction and he set out to change the world as a missionary, regardless of the cost. Furthermore, the pain and suffering that Paul, formerly known as Saul, struggled through was intense. His passion and love for the Lord and building the Church during the 1st Century led him to imprisonment, chains, and eventually his martyrdom. Paul had this to say toward the very end, right before he was killed:

"But none of these things move me; nor do I count my life dear to myself, so that I may finish my race with joy, and the ministry which I received from the Lord Jesus, to testify to the gospel of the grace of God." (Acts 20:24)

It is our deepest and clearest call to serve the Lord. I am not quite sure if I could hear His voice so well or so distinctly today, all of these years later, if I hadn't felt that great absence from God or undergone such hardship. Who knows, it is an ongoing mystery. Though, what I do know for sure is where God has taken me, and I want to highlight this part because the same can be true for you.

It is extremely valuable to understand where you have been and to recall those times in your life in order to better conceptualize where you are now and where God is taking you in the future. He has taken me through the fire and has led me to a place I never could have dreamt of. The same can be true for you as you prevail and weather the storm. You can get through whatever it is that you currently face and you can be led into a new promise for your life. My hope is that you believe that if the Lord can do it for me, He can and will do it for you. Know that I am praying for you right now that you cling to the promise of life that is in Jesus Christ.

Billions of people over the centuries have questioned, wondered, and debated over religion and what tradition and faith is the truth. For me it boils down to this and is quite simple. No other faith tradition or religion has a God who came down and took on human flesh, was willing to walk with us, live through all of the trials and tribulations of life, and then sacrifice Himself on a Cross so that we might live for all eternity. Christ gets it and understands our humanity because he was human and divine, and in lowering himself he was able to experience fully what it is to be human in order to raise us up to share with him the promise that he gained by the power of the Cross. What I hope and pray you realize is that the victory has already been won over the grave. Death has no sting because the grave can no longer hold us down. By His very blood that He shed on the Cross, you and I are set free. The most beautiful and profound thing is that our Lord would have done it solely for you alone. If you were the only person to ever exist, He would have chosen to die for you out of great love. Now that's what I call amazing grace and transformative power. That is redemption and with that kind of force for you, nothing can stop you. With the resurrection power charging through your bones and firing up your spirit, you are undefeatable and have supernatural abilities and limitless potential.

Remember, you and I are children in and of the light. We are meant to walk in the light and not in darkness. Ask for the Spirit to lead you, to strengthen you, and to show you the way. There are cheerleaders in the Saints encouraging you on. Now is the time, do not wait until tomorrow. Take His hand as it reaches out to you and walk by faith, living as a child of the light; "Behold, now is the accepted time; behold, now is the day of salvation." (2 Corinthians 2:6). It is never too late to begin again!

Today can be a new day for you. The sun rises and new opportunities are abounding. Do not wait any longer or go through life alone. We were made for relationships. Take a moment to think about and recall some of the most joyous and love filled times of your life. Who was there? What was the setting? How old were you? What was taking place? Why did you feel so whole and so complete? Now, that is what God desires for you and it is what he longs for you to have. In the eye of the storm when things are out of control and the winds are swirling around you, He does not want you to be afraid. God wants you to have that inner peace and that assurance that you are going to be more than okay. You will come out of this on top and you will still have joy welling up inside of you; for no one and nothing can take it away. The light, the cracks of light in our lives, are the memories of each moment that was good. Each happening and thing we can be grateful for. The light is made of the very people, each place, particular opportunities, and most of all the turnaround that we have seen. Your past does not determine your destiny or designate the future you will and can have. As we take a look back and reflect, and see clearly all of the blessings that have come to us and the many small and big moments that we have been through, it puts things in perspective. As the saying goes, "hindsight is 20/20." The difficulties which we have overcome can be used as jet fuel to launch us off the runway. They can be used to encourage us in knowing that this new life we desire is possible. The light fills us up within and we know that we are more than conquerors. As warriors, we can carry on. And as warriors that is exactly what we do. We continue to battle.

"I am the resurrection and the life. He who believes in Me, though he may die, he shall live." (John 11:25)

-Jesus Christ

CHAPTER 7: From Death to Resurrection

"Then Jesus called out in a Loud voice, 'Father, into your hands I commend my spirit.'" Luke 23:46

Friday Moments

In life we inevitably will face challenges; however, sometimes we come up against something that is unimaginable, unfair, agonizing, and excruciatingly painful. How can an all powerful, all loving God allow for this to happen? Why me? Why now? Why is all of this heartache and pain crashing down on me? When will it stop? Will it ever? What did I do to deserve this? How can this be?

Life is full of Friday moments. Some of those Friday moments are manageable, while others seem as if we will never be able to overcome them. Jesus faced Friday just like you and me. He even went as far as to ask His Father to "allow this cup to pass, not my will but yours be done." Christ was whipped and scourged. They brutally beat and mocked him and put on his head a crown of thorns. Our Lord was forced to carry His own cross for miles. He became so exhausted that He needed help to carry it to Calvary. Along came Simon of Cyrene, the man who helped Jesus carry the cross. Then, Christ was nailed to the tree, spikes being driven into His hands and His feet. He bled and bled and was in excruciating pain. He hung there and endured buffets and spitting. Later they would pierce Him with a sword in His side. At last, He cried out to God and then He gave up His Spirit. Friday, is now known as "Good Friday." What was good about this day? A horrifying, horrible, unbearable, terrible, evil, and awful day. Where was the good anyway? Well, it was coming. What Friday moment are you facing? What Friday moments have you faced?

In life we are all going to face Friday moments. These times of "death" and instances of evil and hardship will knock on our door. Although this has happened, and we will face Friday moments again in the future, remember, that this is not the end. If the story ended with Friday for Jesus, there would have been NO good that came of it at all! The devastation, the pain, the suffering, the agony, and the sacrifice would have been for nothing. Per contra, the good news of the Gospel and the good news for you and me is that the story did not and does not end there.

We are stretched and tested in life. Jesus was tested and He suffered greatly. There are Friday moments and there are desert moments that appear for us. But not one of these is impossible to overcome. Not one of these is something that with the power of almighty God working in your life you cannot conquer. Long before His passion and crucifixion, the Lord was in the desert for 40 days and 40 nights. At the end of His time there, the Devil tempted Him, but he did not give in:

"Then Jesus was led by the Spirit into the desert to be tempted by the devil. He fasted for forty days and forty nights,* and afterwards he was hungry. The tempter approached and said to him, "If you are the Son of God, command that these stones become loaves of bread." He said in reply, "It is written: 'One does not live by bread alone, but by every word that comes forth from the mouth of God.'" (Matthew 4:2-4)

Pastor Joel Osteen suggests that Friday moments are like a bow and arrow. The more tension, the more strain, the more we are pulled back, the further we can and will be launched into a new direction of our destiny. Jesus had to endure the cross so He could conquer the grave. Without the suffering, there would have been no glory. The Lord had to die and descend into hell to triumph over death and open up the gates of everlasting life! Friends, often in life, the very problems that press on us and attempt to cause us to be defeated, are the things that when we dig our heels in and fight through, will lead to our greatest victories.

Whether our Friday moment comes via a storm and raging sea, a poor choice that we make, an unexpected diagnosis with our health, a horrific event that happens within our family or by means of temptation, we must be ready and be well equipped for the battle. It is critical for us to be prepared by putting on the armor of God and calling on the Lord for help when we need it. As it says in James 1:12 "Blessed is the man who perseveres in temptation, for when he has been proved he will receive the crown of life that he promised to those who love him."

Life is full of trials and difficulties. But God can, will, and does make beauty from the ashes. After the Friday moment is upon us, after we are facing and staring it in the eyes, we can run or we can fight. After we know this is, and will continue to be an uphill battle and we must reach deep down inside to overcome this thing, the fire will become inflamed. When we choose to not give up and to not give in, when we choose life and do not submit to this being the end, then we will have to cling to our faith, battle, pray, and wait.

Waiting in the Tomb

Friday moments, like that brutal day endured by our Lord, lead to death. Our lives can be upended, we can be crushed, and even destroyed. Sometimes the happenings of life with their severity can completely empty us both physically and spiritually. But remember that this is not the end. Now we enter the tomb and wait. Waiting is not easy. Most people are not the best when it comes to patience. If you are, that is amazing, but having to be still and not know how when it will happen is hard. That is why they say that patience is a virtue. Often in our own lives we do not know how long it will take or how long it will be until things get better. How many days will have to pass before our situation improves. Days, weeks, months go by and we must continue to stay as strong and as positive as possible. Our hope remains and it must because if we lose hope we lose everything. So, we keep on praying, we believe, and we wait longer.

They laid Jesus' body in the Tomb and Mary, His mother, wept. Jesus expressed right before He gave up His spirit, "It is finished."

He finished it so that we always had another opportunity, another chance and another way to rise from the graves of life. Our faith allows us to be resurrected in our own lives. For He said, "I am the way, the truth, and the life," and the Lord promised that we would not only have life here on earth to the full, but forever in the world to come. So the hope remains.

Remember, that we do not live for a Kingdom of this world. This is a hard notion to understand and call to mind, especially during the trials of life. Our world and what we do on a regular basis is all we tangibly know and it is all that is truly certain. So how can we keep in the forefront of our minds that this life is as valuable and important as it is, this life is only the beginning. I believe that during our toughest days being able to understand this concept will actually lighten the load slightly and can alleviate some of the pain. Day by day as we wait and we continue to call upon the Lord, He is refining us like gold tested in fire... "And I will bring the third part through the fire, and will refine them as silver is refined, and will try them as gold is tried: they shall call on my name, and I will hear them: I will say, It is my people: and they shall say, The Lord is my God." (Zacharia 13:9) The Lord is taking our setbacks and working in the Heavens behind the scenes. It is only a matter of time before He turns those trials into set ups for a brighter future. This is probably why Paul urged the Corinthians to pay heed when he uttered these powerful words, "Therefore, we are not discouraged; rather, although our outer self is wasting away, our inner self is being renewed day by day." (2 Corinthians 4:16)

Paul was indeed shipwrecked, abandoned, tortured, and put in prison as we discussed previously and yet all the while he stayed the course understanding that "to live is for Christ and to die is gain." (PHL 1:21) and that He could "Do all things through Christ who strengthens." (PHL 4:13) On our own we can do quite a bit, but with the transformative power of God working in our lives, we can overcome and grow into so much more. All we have to do is call on the name of the Lord who promised He would be there with us and "not leave you or forsake you." He promised and did send us the Holy

Spirit, our advocate to help us, teach us, and guide us through ALL things. We are never alone and God's promise and life in Christ shall not cease; for He achieved victory over death through the blood of His cross. We must believe and continue to carry that cross and walk by faith each day.

As we patiently wait, it really boils down to one word that we will discuss later on in great detail, trust. For now I will share with you a small nugget on trust that has helped me in the waiting room of life. Proverbs 3:5-6 assures us that we must "Trust in the LORD with all your heart, and lean not on your own understanding; in all your ways acknowledge him, and he will make your paths straight." This trust is a huge step. It took me many many years to truly trust the Lord fully. As human beings we want to be in control, we want to steer the ship. It is not easy when the wind is taken out of our sails and the boat starts vearing in a different direction. We are used to and desire to have the wheel and to go where we want to go and when we desire to go there. It is scary and unpleasant when the tides rise, the waves come crashing in and we are taking on water. Like a sailor at sea, it is not time to panic, but instead to hold onto what we know for sure. We must not only trust ourselves and stay as calm as possible, but we must trust the Lord to provide and carry us through. He is our motley crew that will not ever abandon us. As the saying goes, "Let go and let God." I encourage you to allow Him to take the wheel. He can and will calm the storm in your life and your trust will give you strength. In doing so this will allow your anxiety to quell, while God makes a way to safety.

Resurrection power & Redemption

As we emphasized earlier, Jesus won victory. Without the cross and death, there could not have been a resurrection and new life. As you and I now have seen, without the pain and the suffering there is no glory or redemption. Listen to the words of Jesus after He died, was in the tomb for three days, and rose from the dead:

"Jesus told her, "I am the resurrection and the life; whoever believes in me, even if he dies, will live, and everyone who lives and believes in me will never die. Do you believe this?" (John 11:25-26)

Do YOU believe this? Do you and I truly believe that He is the life? Our Lord wants us to have this life now and forever. Life is good. Life is so good. Once, I was on vacation at what is known as America's family resort, Ocean City, New Jersey. As we walked the boardwalk after a fantastic day in the sun, swimming in the brisk ocean waters, and playing sports on the sandy beach, we stopped inside a small shop. Typically we will browse the stores on the waterfront, year after year just out of nostalgia. This has been part of the family tradition during the time we share together on vacation and then often we will go to get some ice cream before heading back to the house we rented. This particular instance was slightly different. I am not really a fan of shopping unless I truly need something; however, on occasion I will spring for a nice item, but it has to be truly worth it in my mind. On that evening, a shirt caught my eye. It was a turquoise color and had a surfer cartoon character smiling on the front. In the center of the image were the few simple, yet powerful words inscribed that read, "Life is good." That T-shirt was something I needed. I quickly took it off the rack and after paying for it, I knew it was more than a "talking T-Shirt." For me that message really conveyed what this is all about. Life is truly good. God created us for a good life. Life is not easy, but still the good remains and prevails, time and time again. Sometimes we need a whisper, a reminder, an encouraging message, a book, a homily, scripture, or a T-shirt to keep us going and stay on track.

Our God not only wants us to be victorious, He wants us to triumph and be filled with life in its fullest capacity here as we reside on earth. We are overcomers and I cannot accentuate this enough, the same power that raised Jesus from the grave is within you and me. After death comes new life and new forms of creation. We see this in nature all of the time or in the cycle of life in our human families. The rain falls and the fields are watered. The sun shines and the grasses and crops are nourished. They grow and they yield a harvest. The farmer cuts them down and they produce food for animals and people alike. In between that process, there are times of drought and a lack of sunshine. Pollutants will fill the air, yet the crop still grows. Sometimes the harvest is ripe earlier than expected. At other times it takes longer because of the challenges the farmer and the crop endured. Yet, in the end there is something good to eat.

A life enters the world. The child grows and becomes an individual, able to think on his or her own and to make decisions. One goes through ups and downs, good times and bad. The child works hard and finds his or her purpose. Children grow up and begin a family of their own. Life progresses and that person grows old and then dies. A person's legacy lives on as one's children raise the next generation and the cycle continues. Life lasts and remains. Recall the words of St.Paul to the Corinthians during their days of uncertainty and doubt:

"Therefore if anyone is in Christ, they are a new creation: old things are passed away; behold, all things are made new." (2 Corinthians 5:17)

We always have another chance with Christ in our life. It is never over until our final hour. We are never too far gone to make a comeback. The Lord our God will decide that moment in time when we breathe our final breath, but until then we muster up the strength to move on. We shall not be afraid. We have so much life to live and so much good that is in our future. The blessings are going to abundantly come our way because this truly is the day that the Lord has made.

A Man of God and person of great faith, Matthew Kelly, who created Dynamic Catholic and has written a multitude of books to encourage others in their life journey by saying the following:

"I think we have to ask ourselves: What part of your life needs to be raised from the dead? Because without a Messiah, without a Savior, without a resurrection, death was pretty final and pretty depressing. But Jesus comes along and says—hold on a minute—even death holds amazing possibilities. And so there might be some aspect of your life that is dead or almost dead or not working out, and I think today is a great day to turn to Jesus and say: Listen, Jesus, I really need you to resurrect this part of my life."

The apostles went to the tomb and it was empty. This was because the suffering and death was done with and life was in store. Only the Lord can do this in our lives. When we allow Him in and unlock the door of our heart, His mercy and grace floods us with great love and transforms us. We then can have power over any darkness in our life, power to break chains of addictions, power to heal and to be forgiven. We have the power to overcome!

On graduation day in May of 2010, I felt on top of the world. I had radically been transformed and the rest of my life was ahead for the taking.

CHALLENGE #3: Waiting for Rebirth

We have all faced disastrous moments in our lives. There have been times when the darkness of Friday and the Cross has been much too heavy to bear. The third challenge is to embrace the suffering we are enduring and turn it over to God. Take a few minutes in quiet prayer today or the next time you go to church and hand over that pain to the Lord. Ask Him to carry your burdens and to lighten your load. Wait patiently because better days are coming, resurrection is in store.

"As long as you live, keep learning how to live."

-Seneca

CHAPTER 8: Nunc Coepi

Begin Again

As we journey through life and as I share my story with you, it is my hope to encourage everyone out there that it is never too late. The Lord knows what you and your family are going through. He loves you and His outstretched arms are waiting for you to return.

I was recently at a dynamic and powerful faith conference in Phoenix Arizona to ring in the New Year and new decade of 2020. I went out west with a bunch of my close friends to watch the ball drop and to light a spark in my own faith life. After hearing how amazing this conference was called "SLS," I thought I would give it a shot, what did I have to lose? While out there in the valley of the sun, we celebrated daily mass with nearly 10,000 young people, there were over 400 priests and 80 bishops present. It was a tremendously powerful experience to listen to compeling talks that fired me up and gave me tools to go out and lead others closer to the Lord.

One evening an unexpected guest came to the main stage to give an encouraging message and to share a testimony. As we waited in our seats to see who this featured guest speaker would be, I thought to myself about my own life and my own story. Everyone has something to share and something to tell. Whether we are rich or poor, young or old, male or female, regardless of race, ethnicity or any other difference; we all have a story. Walking out onto the stage was Pro Bowl quarterback and Future Hall of Famer, Philip Rivers of the San Diego Chargers. The crowd rose to their feet and gave Philip a standing ovation before he even uttered a single word. They did so out of great respect for someone who had accomplished so much in his career as a pro football player and was humble enough to come to share with us some things about his own faith during the offseason. In between the hashes, Rivers was a legend on the football field. Growing up, and for nearly the past two decades, I have watched

Rivers light up the gridiron tossing the pigskin for nearly 60,000 yards and 400 Touchdowns. But what is more impressive than all of that greatness on the field as an athlete was Philip's desire to share his story and faith with us.

Philip has lived by the motto "Nunc Coepi" for many years. He explained to us that the meaning in Latin literally states, "Begin Again." How important and powerful is that for us all to remember. Life is full of moments. Some are more favorable than others. If we keep this mindset each morning when our eyes open and we "Begin again," then we can and will see. With this mentality, we can and will experience victory. For a quarterback, especially a signal caller under center in the NFL, this mindset is imperative. 198 times during his career with the Chargers, Philip RIvers has thrown an interception. Every one of these times he inherently passed the ball to the wrong team and cost his own ball club a chance to score or even win the game. In life we will face turnovers. We will make mistakes that can be costly. A "defender" might come in between our plans and intercept what we had going on or upend what we were set out to do, but stay the course.

Like in football, so is the game of life. Philip reminded us that there is still time on the clock and we can indeed Begin Again. This is one of the major reasons why Philip has had such tremendous success in his career and is such a great leader. I thought about this again during NFL free agency. A few months after hearing his message to a crowd of thousands of young people in a convention center, I was sitting in my living room watching him live out this powerful message in its greatest form. After 16 seasons with the San Diego Chargers, his time for the Bolts has come to an end. The team no longer desired him to lead their franchise. Philip could have been bitter about the team not wanting him back. He could have questioned the Lord about this. Instead, he fell back on Nunc Coepi and trusted. Philip would enter the 2020 season as the starting quarterback for the Indianapolis Colts. Just like that, he packed his bags and headed for the midwest. Philip has long desired to win a Super Bowl title, which did not happen for him in San Diego. Who knows, maybe these new beginnings, this "Begin Again" for him will result in #17 hoisting the Lombardi trophy as a Colt. Time will tell. Regardless of the outcome for Philip and his personal career, there is something we clearly have learned from him. Nothing in life is perfect. Many times and in many ways we will have to start over, and that is.

So what does Nunc Coepi mean for you? How can this montra impact your life and your situation? How may this mindshift allow you to realize that today is a new day and that the beginning you desire is right before you? As for me, I turned to the Lord. I knew that after going through all I had gone through in high school, I needed to change some things and I needed to begin again. I got that fresh start when I left the 518 for the 315 and began a new chapter at Le Moyne. I knew that I must spend quality time in the scriptures daily and focus on the positives that were going for me. I began to go to mass more regularly, spend time with the Lord and eventually every day received the Eucharist because that is what I needed. I decided I move on from the dark past that haunted me and tried to rob me of a future. I embraced the opportunity to live out Nunc Coepi because after all, sometimes starting again is all we can do. Personally, I centered my life around the Lord fully, walking daily doing all I could to serve Him. I sought out His will and continue to do so till this day because in Christ I am a new creation. God spared me from the darkness. He rescued me from death and brought me to life again.

When you get a second chance it is pivotal that you embrace it. It was as if I got to trade in the bad hand for a new deck of cards. I was entering a new game and no one could tell me otherwise. My shades were still on, but I was walking taller than ever before. Kanye West was right in his hit song *Stronger*... "N-now th-that that don't kill me, can only make me stronger. I need you to hurry up now. 'Cause I can't wait much longer." Air in the lungs, eyes open, ready to fly. Time to get after it again. When it doesn't go your way or you fail because it is not a matter of if, but when...remember, *Nunc Coepi*, I begin again. Let that restart be better than the last because one day we will eventually get there.

"We are shaped by our thoughts, we become what we think."

-Gautama Budha

CHAPTER 9: Change the Channel

Come on! Did we have to watch this show again? When would it be my turn to pick what was on the television for the night. It was time to relax and kick back on the sofa after a long day. *Tiger King*, *The Bachelor*, or another Hallmark movie. What would it be this time? Sorry ladies. That stuff is not my cup of tea or should I say bottle of beer for that matter. Life with no sports is rough, I am just saying. Right about now I could really go for an epic NBA matchup between LeBron and Steph Curry or even a college basketball game would do. Oh yeah, that's right Caronavirus cut down the nets in Atlanta, cancelling March Madness and the Final Four. As if that wasn't enough, it struck out Major League Baseball and even sank the Masters Golf Tournament. In all seriousness though, watching some sports would totally wet my appetite right about now. Everyone can use some mind numbing stimuli to take us away for even a little while.

Every day millions of people around the world turn on their television set as a form of entertainment and to gain insight. The remote control is a powerful tool in any household. Who controls the channels and what is being watched is often highly coveted. Whether it is the morning, afternoon, or night, the TV is on. Undoubtedly, television gives us a great deal of important information. A connection is made in our brain between what we watch, what we hear, and then what we think about and eventually do. Many times as a kid growing up I would turn on the TV and watch the big game. It could be an NBA playoff matchup, the Final Four, Super Bowl, or World Series. Sometimes it wasn't even a high stakes game, but was a regular season contest. I would watch and take it all in. I took in the sights and the sounds. I could feel the energy in the stadium or arena. The crowd was yelling, signs were being held, cheering was going on. A player scored a big basket, made a touchdown, hit a homer, or did something spectacular and memorable. I wanted to be like them. It left a mark in my mind.

As a kid I was the biggest sports enthusiast. After the game was over I would go outside and pick up whatever ball and play whatever sport I had just been watching. Often I put on the jersey of that particular team or superstar that I wanted to emulate. I pretended to be Michael Jordan, Peyton Manning, Ken Griffey Junior, and Wayne Gretzki. For a while in my life I thought I could be Allen Iverson on my black top as a backyard basketball legend. I wore the Sixers jersey and shorts, had the AI shoes, and even made an arm sleeve that read, "THE ANSWER." Having watched Iverson before and then taking it right to the court it left a direct impact on my performance. Imagining I was the great Sixer ball player and believing I was a superstar like the Philly product, made me shoot better than I normally could. I guess I overlooked AI's infamous rant about practice where he said, "We talkin' about practice man. Not the game. Not the game. We talkin' about practice." I guess the perennial ALL Star didn't feel that practice was all that necessary at that point in his career. As for me, practice was king. What I want to highlight is that because I imagined the great Iverson in my mind and envisioned his killer crossover and moves, I developed more game. My moves were becoming faster, smoother, and my cross over more deadly. I was invincible and largely due to the fact that the thought or power of positivity was running through my mind, time and time again. I truly believed it. I had found *The Answer* and I was ready to ball hard.

See, our minds are our greatest tool and yet they can also be our worst enemy. The mind is an organ that either controls us or we control it. When the mind controls us we lose and are quickly defeated. When we control our thoughts and pull the strings of our mind, the brain becomes our greatest ally. There is a scientific connection between the mind and the rest of the body. The cerebral cortex, cerebellum, upper lobe and other parts of the brain need to be firing on all cylinders to operate correctly. This often happens without us even having to think. We do complete so many daily tasks from memory due to the fact that we have programmed our brain.

Considering as much as we can do to program our brain for the good and use it to our advantage, unfortunately, we fall into the trap of bad thoughts. Negative ideas and detrimental concepts tend to leak their way into our minds every so often, especially when we are feeling the blues. Instead of blocking those thoughts out, we, from time to time, allow them to sneak in. For some strange reason, we then latch onto those thoughts and mindsets and they begin to pollute our brain. If we are not careful, they will mess up the programming in our minds. What we must do is change the channel.

A number of years ago as I was driving in my car, I turned on the radio and was searching for something good and positive to listen to. I came across the Joel Osteen radio show and he was giving a sermon on changing the channel of our minds. The following minutes were filled with this concept and idea that I have since done my best to emulate and utilize in order to keep the right frame of mind. There is great power in positive thinking and we must have our guard up against any negativity that tries to sneak in. The following is what I have learned from this sermon and I hope that you can take away some valuable pieces that will keep your mind free and clear of debris and in a clear and peaceful state.

When I am watching TV if it is something I do not like or is not positive, something that is disturbing or just not to my liking, what do I do...I pick up the remote and change the channel. Why would I continue to watch? It is as easy as one click of the button. Joel suggested that our minds are like a computer system. It is important to take care of them and foster positive thoughts, build upon pure and healthy ideas. If a negative thought comes our way we just have to change the channel. Viruses will from time to time impair a computer system and it is not able to function at optimal running speed or perform at its highest level. The anti virus software is the protective wall that fights against and battles any impending bad thing that comes into the central system of the computer.

For us, we must have the ability to change the channel. We cannot allow negative thoughts to take control. Thoughts lead to action, and action over time leads to habits. Habits then lead us down a path. The path we want and desire is one that is full of life, happiness, joy, positivity and goodness. Yest, if we are not careful as to guard our minds, we can go down a rabbit hole that is lined with nothing but the opposite. St. Paul knew this so well when he was speaking to the Romans, "Do not conform yourselves to this age but be transformed by the renewal of your mind, that you may discern what is the will of God, what is good and pleasing and perfect." (Romans 12:2)

The mind is central to our path in life as it is connected to the total functionality of the rest of the human body. When our mind is right, our body can operate well and in a healthy manner. If our brain is not working correctly or if it is muddled up with junk, harmful thoughts, and unfavorable ideas, it will impact the overall wellness of our physical nature. Not to mention, a poisoned mindset will destroy our mood, our persona, and our ability to function in society. The mind is something that we must take control of and be able to change the channel or reprogram if we notice we are out of sorts. Mindfulness is a practice that we must continue to carry out, as it is a key toward winning in this life and becoming all you and I were created to be.

Decluttering our minds is a practice that meditation and stillness can be so valuable in teaching us to simply be. The great philosopher and guru on mindfulness, Eckhart Tolle, has dedicated most of his life toward teaching people how to be present and not entrapped in their minds. In his books *A New Earth* and *The Power of NOW*, Tolle speaks about the ways that we as humans get attached to things, including becoming attached to the very thought process where ideas race around in our minds. He goes on to explain how being too attached to the past or being too ultra focused on the future leads to anxiety and fear. Depressive states and negativity are more susceptible to infiltrate the human person when they latch onto concepts and create labels and expectations. Eckhart urges his audience to practice the ability to stimulate one's full conscience by noticing thoughts that come and go, whether they are thoughts pertaining to the past or the future, but not holding on to them. Over time, in doing so, he believes that people can be more attuned to what they are experiencing in the present moment and can become fully alive in what he calls the

"NOW." This awakening of consciousness is what frees the human person and allows one to have peace and tranquility. Tolle suggests that this mindfulness and taking control over one's mind, rather than being controlled by it is essential for us as creatures with a conscience. He states that the only thing that is guaranteed to us is the "Now," so it is important for us to be aware and be fully present to live in that moment or reality. After reading his books, I can say that this is certainly challenging in practice; however, I am more aware than ever if I am latching on to past notions or taking my thoughts way too far into the future, and it has allowed me to live more fully in the present moment. This has improved my overall quality of life and has taken away a ton of worry. In addition, being in the so-called "Now," allows me to lose myself in what I am doing and enjoy that experience more freely and openly. This is quite liberating as opposed to constantly watching the clock or thinking about what I must do next. Eckhart is right in saying that the only guarantee we have is what is happening during this moment so it is important for us to be fully alive and fully present to enjoy it.

Personally, I did not have the understanding of how to change the channel earlier in my life. I did not know how to escape the negativity or where to go when these thoughts began many years ago; however, nowI do know. I know how to stop and pray. I know how to change the channel so to speak and do something else that turns the attention and focus from the negative to the positive.

Life enthusiast and inspirational speaker David Goggins explained the mind being the greatest and most essential weapon for the human person. His story is amazing. He grew up in a rough town and did not have much parental support. His dad was absent and his mom worked a couple jobs leaving David to really fend for himself. He had to raise himself basically and did so not out of desire but out of need for survival. David then drifted through life and became depressed. In his depression he resorted to things that were detrimental to his health. He became very obese; however, one day David woke up and decided to change. He joined the Navy and desired to be a seal. A switch flipped in him and he understood that this was not the life he wanted to lead nor was he living up to his full potential.

David was off to BUDS Navy Seal training program, a six month endeavor at the age of 18. It would be either sink or swim. At the time David weighed a whopping 297 pounds and was in no condition to succeed. Some 18 months later, and three full BUD sessions of the most intense training the military and this planet can offer, changed his life. David lost 106 pounds and had endured the most physically and mentally taxing time of his life. He endured, and was now a Seal. More importantly, his mind had been reprogrammed from a cannot attitude to a can do mentality. David has said so many times in his inspirational talks and book *Can't Hurt Me*, that the mind will conform to what it knows. If we do something enough and keep going, if we do not quit, then that becomes our new normal. For David Goggins it was fighting through broken bones and unbelievable pain. It was battling fatigue and not allowing oneself to throw in the towel or as the Seals call it, "Ring the bell," which signifies surrender. David fought and then he fought some more. One Buds training down, a second and he still did not quit. He was able to master his mind and achieve something most people would never imagine attempting.

What will your mentality be? Who do you want to become? What is your ceiling? Chances are that there is so much more untapped potential inside of you! It is time for you to tap into it and get the most out of yourself and this life. Stop throwing yourself a pity party. I know it's hard. I know that the cards you are dealt are unfair and no one should have to go through what you are going through. I get it because I was there. I walked that beat and it nearly took my very life away from me. But somehow and some way I carried on. One must continue to keep going for another hour, another day, another week, another month, another year. You will retrain yourself and your mind and whatever it is that you are facing will become more bearable. Your stamina will build and you will grow in perseverance. The difficulty or issue that you are up against must be entered into fully and when you immerse yourself to full capacity and decide in your mind, "I will win," then you take on a victorious mentality and nothing can stop you. Truly, the only thing or person that can stop you is, well you. If you decide to do it, go through with it, face it, and battle it, you will conquer and you will come out on top. Nevertheless, if you decide you can't, won't, shouldn't, and there is no way, well then that will be your destiny.

The great Henry Ford helped create an efficient assembly line process that led to the first affordable automobile in the United States. It forever revolutionized the world and the way that we travel, making cars accessible to the common man. Now, hundreds of millions of people around the globe get behind the wheel to go from place to place each day. The motor vehicle radically changed the game for transportation, ventures, and quality of life. It is hard to imagine a world without cars. As Ford was creating the new and improved automobile, he stayed super focused. He had a dream and a desire. Throngs of people came out and said things like, "It cannot be done," and "You are wasting your time." The naysayers did not distract Ford from his goal. He set his mind on creating a system of production that would work to manufacture affordable vehicles for all. Most people do not realize that Henry Ford did not succeed the first time he tried. He failed twice in the first seven years of his attempt to reinvent the way cars were produced and made. On the third try he succeeded. So what led him to keep going after the money in his pocket was dry and failure after failure ensued. Well, it was probably the fact that you are not a failure until you quit and stop trying. No matter how hard it is, no matter how many times it takes, it is not a loss until you decide it's over. Henry Ford lived out the montra, "Whether you think you can or you think you cannot, you are right." These words of wisdom are so true. It is you and I who have the power in our minds, with our thoughts to either believe or disbelieve. If you believe it, you will achieve it, if you don't you won't. Now, I finally understand why my mom so often would read to me the story of *The Little Engine that Could*. What one thinks or believes ends up being lived out or it dies. My hope is that every day and with whatever you are attempting to tackle and defeat you think, "I think I can, I think I can." In doing so, you too will stoke that inward fire and gather up enough steam to ascend to the top of the mountain.

Grit and perseverance are imperative for us to battle the war of the mind. Realize there are countless people who achieved greatness before you and for most of them we only know about the glory, not the trials they trudged through to get to the top. Did you know that Walt Disney was fired from the *Kansas City Star* because his editor felt he "lacked imagination and had no good ideas?" 27 Times Dr. Seuss' first book was rejected by different editors until he finally broke through and was given a shot. Abe Lincoln, one of our most iconic presidents, failed in business three times and lost seven campaigns before being elected. Colonel Sanders went door to door trying to sell his chicken to over 1,000 restaurants and was rejected by every single one, only to start his own which became the infamous KFC food chain. And then there is Thomas Edison whose teachers told him he was "too stupid" to learn anything. Edison explained his trial by fire the best as he forged a path to success with great determination, "I have not failed, I have just found 10,000 ways that won't work." Imagine if he would have given up. We would have lost out on the light bulb, phonograph, and the movie camera. Edison's setbacks stimulated his mind so much that they led to new inventions that he had not even thought of originally. Simply amazing. As Michael Jordan, the GOAT of the basketball world (greatest of all time) put it, "I have failed over and over again and that is why I succeed."

When we understand that it isn't a failure until we tap out or give up, then things change in a big time way. The great Yogi Berra, Yankees legendary catcher said, "It isn't over til it's over." The time is still yours. There is more to the story and you can change the game. The outcome is not written in cement, instead it is written in the sand. Waves will come and try to wash them away. Your dreams will seem far off and people or circumstances might attempt to deter you. Stay the course. Keep your mind set on what you desire. You can and you will accomplish your goal if you want to. It is all up to you. It might take longer and be harder than you had initially thought, but that is okay. You have what it takes. Now go out there, set yourself on the course you desire, and take it! Nothing in life that is worthwhile comes easy. Then again, how much sweeter is that victory when we achieve what we desired after putting in the blood, sweat, and tears to get there. Victory or defeat, the choice is yours. It begins every day and it starts with a battle, a war that begins in the mind.

CHALLENGE #4: Positive Thinking

Your fourth challenge is to practice some more mindfulness. There is great power in positive thinking. We can all at times get stuck in a rut and become consumed with negative thoughts. Take five minutes today and if you can a few days a week to quiet your mind. As you did so, concentrate on positive thoughts. What are you looking forward to? What is it that is exciting you right now in life? If you catch yourself thinking about something negative and attaching yourself to it, try your best to change the channel by calling to mind a positive thought.

"It isn't where you came from. It's where you're going that counts."

-Ella Fitzgerald

CHAPTER 10: Starting Lineups

The PA system turned on in full force as the announcer sitting at center court professed to the crowd filled arena, "At guard, standing 6'8" from St. Vincent/St. Mary's High School, number 23, LeBron James!" The fans go wild, as King James runs through the gauntlet of teammates and does a rehearsed customized hand shake with perennial All-Star teammate, Anthony Davis. It is almost game time at Staples Center in Los Angeles California. LeBron is about to take the court again in front of 20,000 fans draped in purple and gold. This scene here in Hollywood is the Mecca of Sports, the grand stage. All of the "showtime" has grown accustomed to the Lakers superstar who has taken over in L.A. James, who desired to get the Lakers back to the glory days of the early 2000s when Shaq and Kobe ran the town, he had big shoes to fill. In the wake of the tragic death of Bryant, LeBron has been extra intentional about personifying the "Mamba mentality" and leading his team from Southern California back to basketball immortality. The goal for the King is always another ring. After all, it seems like no matter what he does, he will always be chasing the ghost of Michael Jordan. Whether it is out in L.A., way down in South Beach for the Heat, or in his home state of Ohio for the Cleveland Cavaliers, James knows what the fan fare is all about. He is ready to not only put on a show for the crowd as one of the world's greatest entertainers, but he is ready to compete for another world championship. Four rings and counting, the King has his eyes set on basketball allure and reaching the pinnacle of hoisting the Larry O'Brien Trophy again.

    LeBron sheds his warm ups and heads to the scorers table. He takes his ceremonial baby powder and sprinkles it in his hands. Then, like he has done for the past 17 seasons, he throws it in the air and the particles create a mist that eventually dissipates into the night. James heads to center court ready for another 48 minutes on the hardwood. As an NBA fan and a follower of LeBron since he was back in high school, it is easy to see his passion for the game of basketball. I know of him, the greatest player in the world, through his play on the court. The stats he stuffs in the box score of the newspaper each night, and the highlights I watch speak volumes to the world about how dominant this man is. I follow him on social media and read articles about his life. I know of LeBron through a particular lens. I do not personally know him. Sure, it would be cool to be one of his "boys" and truly know the man who got the nickname "THE KING" by age 18. Reality is I do not know him and most likely, I never will.

There is a major difference in life when it comes to knowing of someone, and knowing someone. To merely hear the name through association or be able to recall facts, information, or other ideas is one thing. To spend time with, understand, and fully comprehend through a personal relationship a person in their totality, is totally different. Knowing them and walking life with them is far more enriching. See, many of us out there know of Jesus. We have heard the stories from the Bible. We were baptized, we went through Sunday school, made our First Holy Communion, and probably even got confirmed. Most people can tell you that He lived a pretty normal life for the first thirty or so years, being the son of a carpenter named Joseph and that his birth was miraculous as He was born of a Virgin named Mary. We know that He performed many miracles and even is said to have raised people from the dead. We have heard that Jesus suffered and died for our sins and on the third day he rose to new life, which is why Christians celebrate Easter.

To know of Jesus is easy. One may read books, listen to sermons, hear podcasts, watch movies, and attend faith based retreats. To know Jesus and have a personal relationship with Him is a different ball game, which when we enter into it will totally and radically change our lives. See, the Lord knows us, He doesn't just know of us. When we were created every molecule in our body, every chromosome, every hair on our heads, beauty mark, and physical attribute was designed by God. More importantly, every characteristic, every passion, all the desires we have, the struggles we face, our achievements, our past, present, and future, and life in its total essence, is known by our Lord. He knows us better than we could ever even know ourselves.

Then why do I not take the time daily to get to know Him

more and develop that deep and lasting relationship. He calls me to Himself and wants to spend time with me because I am loved as a Child of the most high. This is true for each of us. Introduce yourself to God and get to know Him. Spend ten minutes a day thanking the Lord for all He has blessed you with. Quiet yourself and tell Him what is in your heart. Share with Him your deepest secrets and the things you are struggling with. Lay it all out there for He wants to know. Take time each week to read the scriptures and pray on them. In doing so you will truly come to know Him. Jesus has so much to share with you and so much He desires for you. It is not enough to know about Him. The Lord wants to be your best friend.

As for me, this personal relationship with Jesus and getting to know him well began when I was eleven and went to Hoop Heaven just north of New York City. At the faith based summer basketball camp, I remember Coach Miller talking about how much work it would take to become a college basketball player, let alone to make it to the NBA. He had the opportunity and privilege to coach rising stars at the top basketball camps and showcase tournaments throughout the country and saw firsthand the great talent of players like Michael Jordan, Allen Iverson, Vince Carter, and more before they came to fame. I was in awe of the names he rattled off. What he said after all of the name dropping was profound. Coach Miller said, "Those names are significant, but they do not compare to the name of the real MVP of my life, Jesus Christ." He explained that basketball is great, it is fun, and it teaches us hard work. However, a personal relationship with Jesus will provide so much more. That night at camp we entered the small chapel and heard some scripture, prayed together, and sang some cool interactive Christian songs. It was at that moment that I understood that I knew of Jesus, but I didn't truly know him. I was given a WWJD bracelet (What Would Jesus Do?) that evening. It is the same bracelet I am still rocking to this day, some twenty years later. That night I prayed really hard and asked Jesus to become my friend. I remember telling the Lord that I truly wanted to know Him. I then added in, it would be pretty cool to become a great basketball player too and make it to the collegiate level. Then again, I was eleven and basketball was life.

My brother Brandan and I pictured today as we use our time to give back to kids to coach camps, lighting the spark in others through sports and faith.

Most of the time we pass by strangers and don't really think too much about what they are wearing, unless of course it is really out there or something that catches our eye as a "must" for our wardrobe. Every once in a while when I am exploring a different city on vacation or traveling, I will run into someone who has a very particular t-shirt on. When I see it, the shirt and its message make me smile. "Jesus is my Homeboy," the shirt says. What if this were true? What if you and I allowed Jesus into the inner circle of our lives. What if we talked to Him daily? What if we spent even a quarter of the amount of time with Christ as we do scrolling through our Instagram feed on a daily basis? Our lives would be changed in a tremendous way.

The thing is, when we come to know our Lord and who He really is and what His life was all about, then we can know ourselves more and understand the meaning of life in a greater capacity. It is pretty simple, yet so dense in terms of its value. Take a peanut butter and jelly sandwich. My favorite quick go to snack. My stomach is starting to grumble even thinking about it. Three simple ingredients that take 30 seconds to whip up and you have a high protein filled substance to munch on that packs a big punch. So what is the big deal you say about peanut butter, jelly, and some multigrain bread. Well, if you get to know what are in the ingredients, what they are made up of, the processes for them to go through from farm to table, then you would understand how this is the recipe for a workout warrior to excel in the gym. The peanut butter is high in protein and also contains good essential healthy fats. On the other hand, the jelly consists of natural sugars and carbs to spike glucose levels. Finally, the bread of course is carb heavy and has necessary fiber. All of this combined is eaten and turned into energy for one to be able to crush a gym session.

Knowing verses knowing of. Understanding all that encompasses, verses being able to recite facts. Realizing what makes someone go and what is imperative to him or her. When we invest in time with our Lord the rewards are not just felt on this earth, but they are eternal. I often laugh at the joke a priest friend of mine told me one time and now I recite to others to loosen up the crowd, "Working for God doesn't pay much, but the retirement plan is out of this world."

In all seriousness though, when we know God and have that personal relationship with His Son, Jesus, we will be filled with joy that is unexplainable. It is why Jesus told His disciples, "I have told you these things so that my joy might be in you and your joy be made complete." (John 15:7). When we know the Lord and realize that He knows, cares about, and loves us more than anyone, it turns your deepest sorrows and times of despair into having Hope for a brighter tomorrow. The highs you experience in life become even more heightened and joyful. It is why Jesus continued to talk to his apostles and disciples and said to them, "And this is eternal life, that they might come to know you, the one true God, and Jesus Christ whom you have sent." (John 17:3). As a shepherd knows his sheep so we must know the Lord because He knows His own and calls them each by name.

A friend of mine was over in the middle east spending time in the Holy Land. It is a remarkable place that I hope to go to and visit some day on a pilgrimage. Unless you are a farmer or from that region in the world, you might not have the knowledge or an appreciation for shepherding a flock. My friend wanted to tell me this story when he experienced a shepherd and his flock over near Jerusalem. I thought to myself how this is going to relate to my life. Who really cares about a guy ushering around some animals in a field? As he started the story I could quickly tell that there was something important, some kind of lesson that this was going to teach me, so I listened fully. The shepherd was in a field with his flock and then made a whistle, all of the sheep came running in his direction and gathered in. He did not even have to use his staff. How could that be? In a matter of less than a minute, the hundreds of sheep dispersed in an enormous meadow were now by his side. The shepherd walked and the sheep followed. They had to cross a busy road and get through a densely populated area to venture back to the farm for the night. Although, what happened was there were two more sheep folds crossing at the same exact time.

Now I was thinking this is going to be a disaster, but without missing a beat the shepherd continued to whistle and make his call. Amidst the other two flocks and hundreds of other sheep, countless people in the town outskirts and cars honking, not a single sheep went astray. The shepherd knew his flock and they truly and deeply knew his voice; fully trusting that he would not allow them to be harmed. They had built years of trust and there was a deep foundation for the relationship. I then learned that when they got back to the farm, before he went in for the night, the shepherd did something super important. You know what that shepherd did? He went to every one of those sheep and patted it on the head and said a good word to each one. He even bent down and hugged the young ones and looked them in the eye.

How much more does the Good Shepherd, Jesus Christ, want to guide, protect, and love you and me? The Lord is the Shepherd and He knows us and wants us to know Him:

> "I am the good shepherd. A good shepherd lays down his life for the sheep. A hired man, who is not a shepherd and whose sheep are not his own, sees a wolf coming and leaves the sheep and runs away, and the wolf catches and scatters them. This is because he works for pay and has no concern for the sheep. I am the good shepherd, and I know mine and mine know me, just as the Father knows me and I know the Father; and I will lay down my life for the sheep. I have other sheep that do not belong to this fold. These also I must lead, and they will hear my voice, and there will be one flock, one shepherd. This is why the Father loves me, because I lay down my life in order to take it up again. No one takes it from me, but I lay it down on my own. I have power to lay it down, and power to take it up again. This command I have received from my Father." (John 10:11-18)

Relationships take time, they take work, and they take energy. If you do not know the Lord in this type of way I encourage you to get to know Him. It will change your life forever. If you do know Him that is awesome. Keep investing in that relationship and see where He will take you to heights that are unimaginable.

"We must be willing to let go of the life we planned so as to have the life that is waiting for us."

-Joseph Campbell

CHAPTER 11: Radiant Future

There she was again at the edge of the stage. She looked out into the crowd as all of their eyes were on her. It was show time! Another sold out venue in her worldwide tour. The lights flickered and the audience of more than 40,000 fans screamed at the top of their lungs. Her walk was full of confidence and her voice soared through the night…

"Shine bright like a diamond, shine bright like a diamond.
Find light in the beautiful sea, I choose to be happy.
You and I, you and I, we're like diamonds in the sky.
Shine bright like a diamond, shine bright like a diamond."

Robyn Fenty, the native of Barbados, well known as Rhianna in the music world, reached number one on the billboard charts yet again. Like the theme of her hit #1 song for weeks on end, your future is bright. The possibilities are endless. Only God knows everything that is in store. What is certain is that the trials you faced and overcame are only going to strengthen you and give you wings to soar. They are no longer harmful, but are being used to empower you and to bring about inspiration. Just like diamonds that gain in brilliance the more intense pressure they are under, so it is in our lives. The more we face and the harder it is, the more beautiful and radiant the outcome will be. Not to mention how encouraging we will be to all those we meet. The challenges you faced are now part of your past and they are an important part of your story. Your testimony is part of who you are, and is something that will help someone in their time of need.

I pray that my story inspires you and leads you to know that you are not alone. God cares about you. You are the apple of His eye. Jesus loves you and desires to give you His heart. Our Mother, Mary loves you and wants you to come to her Son for help and protection. This life is not easy. It is hard. It is cruel and unfair. The battles we face are greater than we can imagine. But get ready to shine like a diamond. Stop talking about your problems and start telling those problems how BIG your God is! God has no limits. Even when we are dead, He resurrects us, like He did for Lazarus and gives us new life. Lazarus had been dead for four days and was in the tomb when Jesus came and flipped the situation in a miraculous way. "And when he [Jesus] had said this, he cried out in a loud voice, "Lazarus, come out!" The dead man came out, tied hand and foot with burial bands, and his face was wrapped in a cloth. So Jesus said to them, "Untie him and let him go." (John 11:43-44) It is not over until the Lord says it is over. At that moment because of his mercy and overflowing grace, we will stand in front of the Lord and instead of seeing us and our brokenness, the Father will see the Glory of His Son Jesus, the Resurrected Christ in all splendor. We will truly shine brighter than any diamond.

I believe in you and know you can and will conquer. You are an overcomer. You have the power within you that is necessary to drive your body and soul. Today is the day of redemption. Now is the time to renew and ignite your relationship with the Lord. May the fire of Christ burn in you brightly. You have so much more to live for and so much more to offer. There is only one you. There will never be another you in the history of the world. You have gifts, talents, and a calling. You have a mission to accomplish. Little did I know all those years ago that I would be writing this book. I had no idea what God's plan was going to be for my life. Who would have thought one could go from a second away from death to a joy filled life as a married man. It has been a great blessing for me. Thankfully it did not end. It was not over. Fourteen years later as I write this, it makes sense. Only God can do these amazing things and turn our lives around in such a profound and drastic way.

At Le Moyne College, as you now know, I played basketball. But that wasn't an easy road for either. It wasn't all glory for me on the hardwood, let alone getting there in the first place. It wasn't a continuous euphoria that we felt after bouncing back to defeat Syracuse in the greatest win in program history. My story began with loss and a major defeat. I tried out for the team my freshman year and was cut. Oh no, here we go again, another set back; however, my coach offered me a spot as the team manager. I would help with scouting reports, keeping track of stats, taking care of equipment, and travel. It was really hard to be on the bench in a polo shirt during practice and eventually a suit on game days watching my dream slip away. I began to throw myself a pity party, but then woke up one day and thought next year I will be on this team. I will make the roster. Little did I know that being cut as a freshman, was really a set-up. It was only a matter of time until I would shine! That following spring and summer after the season was over I worked harder than I ever had on my game. The words that motivated me the most were spoken to me by my head coach before I left that summer toward the end of May. He told me don't think about trying out for the team next year, you have no chance of making it. You are not strong enough or quick enough. He said there were no roster spots open. I will be honest I was heated at hearing these words. They were like venom pumping through my veins. I thought to myself, now he just ignited the fire inside of me to do whatever it takes to prove him wrong. That is exactly what I set out to do.

There were countless hours of conditioning, ball handling, and lifting weights. I was shooting 500-700 jump shots a day until my arms could hardly move and then shooting some more. I was working arduously on the blacktop outside of my parents house doing speed and agility drills in the middle of the summer heat. A kid from a small farm town in Germantown, NY was motivated and getting better every day. All of that countless hard work led me to tryouts the following fall. I showed up and my coach looked at me, without saying anything his demeanor said it all. He must have been thinking, why did this kid even decide to show up? Not only did I show up, not only did I land a position on the roster that season, but through hard work and dedication I became the team captain by my senior year. So long for holding other people's jockstraps and only dreaming of wearing the green and gold, I was a Dolphin. We would go on to beat Syracuse during my senior year as I mentioned earlier. This was one of the most exhilarating moments of my life.

As a boy I practically worshipped Syracuse Orange basketball, truth be told, I still do today. The Carrier Dome was filled with over 30,000 screaming fans and Jim Boeheim, one of the greatest and winningest coaches of all time, was calling out the plays. I recall Carmelo Anthony cutting down the nets and winning the first title for the Orange after the greatest run in NCAA history as a freshman. A few months later he would then become the third overall pick in the 2003 draft. Wow! Now I was in the Dome and it wasn't as a fan. I didn't have a ticket for the game, I was the ticket for the game. People were coming to watch me and they wanted to see us play. Now I was lacing them up against future NBA stars and looking down toward the other side of the court about to square off against the team I idolized. I was shaking hands with Coach Boehim and smiling as he grimaced in defeat after we knocked off the number one team in the nation! This is stuff you can't make up. Little did I know that later on in life, God would use my personal story of rising above defeat as a basketball player to speak about perseverance in life and to motivate youth. It has become a platform for me to inspire thousands of kids through my work as a coach, teacher, and camp director over the years. I have also had the privilege for numerous years to speak to college students in hopes of inspiring them through my story and to lead them to become their personal best. Once again another reminder to us that God can bring some good out of every situation and use us as an instrument. Trials and all, what we go through can be used to change the world.

The best thing about a future is it is not yet written. We have the opportunity to be co-authors of our life story. It is as if we are working on the creation of an artistic masterpiece. Each day we come to the studio and chip away at the block that is before us, sculpting it and chiseling every fine detail. Sometimes as we discussed previously, we need to embrace *Nunc Coepi*. We wipe the canvas clean and start again. The future is full of possibility. The past we cannot change. As much as many of us might wish we could go back with a giant eraser and wipe away mistakes, hardship, and the unpleasant moments that came our way as we journey through life, we cannot. What we can do is take a pencil and start writing our future because nothing is permanent. The future can continue to change, and change it will. Write out the next year, five years, twenty five years of your life. What does it look like? What will you be doing? Who will be there and most of all what excites you the most? This is not a mirage like in the desert when someone is sojurning and desperately seeking an oasis to quench their thirst. No, this is attainable. My challenge to you right now is to utilize what David Goggins calls the *Accountability Mirror*. Take some post-it notes and write down your dreams, your goals, your plans, and your desires. Post them up on your mirror so that every day when you look in your own eyes you know what you are striving for. You can see what your finish line says for each race you set out to run. You can visualize and keep in the very forefront of your mind the things that will happen, the future you will live out because you are choosing that path for your life. Start shining bright like a diamond.

See, God knows what your future holds and only He knows how bright and good it will be. Michael Jordan was the greatest of all time. Imagine if he were to have given up after being cut from his varsity team many years ago. The set back is a set up to fuel your desire and to allow you to become all you were created to be. You are a champion. I am not talking about winning six titles like the great Air Jordan or cutting down the nets in the NCAA tournament. I am talking about a greater championship than that. Those things will pass, but your life is filled with so much potential and opportunity if you just keep going and do not give up.

After earning my masters degree in teaching I went on to educate inner city youth in Albany in one of the poorest and most troubled areas in the state. God blessed me with a great opportunity to teach at KIPP Tech Valley and for the next eight years I dedicated my life to providing hope, inspiration, and a choice filled future to my students in my English classes. When I took the job I did not know how it would go or how hard it would be. I did not realize that I would impact hundreds of kids each year and some of them I would mentor later on in life. I share this with you because there is a plan and greatness lies inside. We must do our best to plant seeds of greatness in the next generation. It is our responsibility to cultivate a culture of love and respect, and of making the world a better place. You never know the impact you can have on others.

Now I have since moved on from the classroom. Nunc Coepi, I begin again. As I sit in my office at NOVUS Clothing Company and work in the business world of custom apparel, I am excited to see where God will take me next. As I journey on in all senses of the word, I have been taken to the streets and dumps of Mexico City to feed the homeless and share Christ's love with the poorest of the poor. I have been blessed with the opportunity to go to Nebraska and serve on the Native American reservation with the Winnebego and Omaha tribes. I never thought I would head to prisons on a weekly basis to lead faith sharing and bible studies, as well as give talks to the masses at retreats for the incarcerated. It excites me to dream and imagine what will be in the next year of my life, let alone the next fifty or however long I am blessed to live. Only God knows.

At my business headquarters where I now work for NOVUS Clothing Company bringing custom sports apparel to people around the world.

Teaching at **KIPP** Tech Valley Charter School in Albany, NY for eight years was amazing. Having a chance to educate and inspire young people was truly special.

So what will your future hold? Who do you want to become? What do you desire to do? It is all possible and can and will happen if you want it to. My question to you is how bad do you want it? Will you do whatever it takes? Do you believe it is possible? Now it is time for you, like it was for me, to begin again. God knows what we desire. He knows what is in the very depths of our heart as the Psalmist wrote, "Delight yourself in the Lord and He will grant you the desires of your heart." (Psalm 37:4) We were created for a purpose and have a mission in this world. Our time on earth is not coincidence or chance. We have a density and we have a legacy to fulfill. I first heard that scripture from the book of Psalms from the great Oprah Winfrey. Oprah, wow the woman who gave away TVs and cars in excitement on her show. No, there is a lot more depth to it than that. Maybe you don't know her story, or maybe you do. She was abused as a young child. She was unwanted and had an extremely tough childhood. The cards and world were stacked against Oprah growing up in the projects and inner city. Her life was destined for disaster. That was what the world might think or say, but God clearly had different plans for her life. She has used her story, her power of influence, her voice and now her celebrity status to bring hope and impact millions across the globe with her talk show. She became a great philanthropist and has a foundation dedicated to serving and helping the poor and children in Africa and so many other causes around the world.

    The baby boy was on the way. An excited mom was about to have her new child born into the world. Another little miracle had happened on that sunny day! That baby she named Timothy. Now, 33 years later, Tim is a pro athlete who uses his platform to change the world. After multiple national championships and a Heisman trophy at the University of Florida, Tim went on to play professional football with the Denver Broncos and a number of other teams. Most recently, he has worked extremely hard to rise to the AAA level with the New York Mets, hoping to crack through into the Big Leagues during the 2020 season. What is most impressive about Tim is not his great athleticism, but that he has numerous hospitals and orphanages in the Philippines, and he developed a foundation that serves those with developmental disabilities and handicaps. Tebow created a Night to Shine, where hundreds of thousands of special needs children around the world are able to experience a prom where they are crowned King and Queen. Tim has written numerous books, is a regular host on College Gameday on ESPN, and he continues to tell his story to encourage people across the globe. Tebow was another diamond in the rough.

Michael Jordan, Dan Jason, Oprah Winfrey, Tim Tebow. What do we all have in common? We each have a story. Each of us has a past that included trials and difficulty. It is faith that carried us on. We each had trust and belief that our futures were bright, and this motivated each of us. Now is your time to shine. Now it is your chance to pave your future and leave a legacy. Tim Tebow discusses the value of legacy by saying the following, "Eventually, when our life is over there will be a tombstone. On it there will be the year we were born and the year we died. In between the years will be a dash. What do you want your dash to represent?" So, what do you want your legacy to be? What will you do to impact one person, one day at a time, to make someone's life better? Will you leave this world better off than when you entered it? I sure hope so and I know you can. The great Jackie Robinson broke the color barrier in baseball. He would go on to smash many records. Robinson won a World Series for the Brooklyn Dodgers and then became the first player to ever have his number retired across the game. But see Jackie Robinson would be the first to tell you that all the pomp and circumstance means nothing. The awards, accolades, and even being the most famous person in the United States at one point during his heyday is pointless when compared to how we must live in order to affect the lives of others. Jackie Robinson had worked really hard with civil rights leaders and activists. Robinson showed that the meaning of life was found in the very fabric of how one chose to impact the lives of other people. For me Robinson is a hero for living that powerful message out and reminding us of what matters most in life.. Thus, the challenge is before each of us. Make a big splash, take some chances, and be an overcomer. Use your story and your past. The hurt and the pain can now be used to your advantage. When called upon, share your testimony and see how others will be inspired.

Human beings are naturally scared of vulnerability. Yet, it is when we let our guard down and are willing to share the difficult things we have faced, and the painful experiences, that we become more real to others. Unfortunately, we live in a day and age where social media rules and controls the world. One cannot go a day, let alone an hour, without being influenced or infiltrated with the latest Instagram post, tweet, Facebook update, or Snapchat story. It is the world we now live in; however, the danger is that most people on these social platforms put up a facade that does not tell the truth. The picture is painted in a rosey way and everyone's life appears to be "perfect." We all know this is not the case and yet we still get sucked into the vacuum of comparisons.

Real truth and change, real impact and encouragement can be made when we are honest. When we open up ourselves and let that guard down to become vulnerable. When we share with people intimately the struggles, the challenges, the heartbreak of our lives it is not easy. Yet, after we get over the uncomfortable nature, it allows us to connect on much a deeper level. We see one another eye to eye and into the very depths of our hearts. Our brokenness is not something to be ashamed of. What we went through is not something to hide. The old saying, "Don't reveal the skeletons in your closet," doesn't have to be. Instead, we are able to connect in a way that was not possible before. Trust is built and then people are able to share what is on their minds and what they are facing. This is not possible if we do not open up first and create a time and a space that is safe. This encounter we have with others is so good and beautiful because it will free them from being alone. It will emancipate them from being afraid and allows people to realize that they too will overcome whatever they face in time. There have been people who have gone through it before and there is a community who cares about them, namely the Church called the Body of Christ.

CHALLENGE #5: Future Aspirations

Today's challenge is for you to dedicate ten minutes toward your future. Despite what has happened in your past, you have a bright future ahead of you. What do you want your future to hold? Write down your future aspirations and desires. We will come back to this list later on. For now, just let the pen flow and let your mind run wild with hope and how your future life can unfold to bring you some real joy.

"Life isn't about finding yourself. Life is about creating yourself."

-George Bernard Shaw

CHAPTER 12: Run Your Own Race

> "Do you not know that those who run in a race all run, but only one receives the prize? Run in such a way that you may win." (1 Corinthains 9:24)

It was evening and the sun had just set. The fans were going crazy in the main stadium and there was a clear buzz in the air. He stepped up to the starting line with one event left in the Rio games of the 2016 Olympics. It was the 4X100 meter medley relay. Usain Bolt was about to make even more history. In a matter of minutes, from this moment as he approached the track, he would be crowned a champion again. A record 9th gold medal would be draped around his neck. The world's fastest man was on top of the pyramid once again, earning a place in Olympic history.

When I think of runners the first one that comes to mind is the greatest sprinter of all time, Usain Bolt. There are other legends that graced this sport throughout history like Michael Johnson, Carl Lewis, and Jesse Owens. However, none of them was able to do what Bolt has done. The Jamaican athlete is in a league of his own, possibly his own stratosphere in the world of running. Breaking records is an understatement for Bolt. It is more like shattering records. His name is the most fitting of any that I have ever heard for a competitor in their respective sport. It was as if he was destined to run. Well, in fact he was.

In life it is critical that we run our own race. We must stay in our lane. What made Usain Bolt so lethal was that he never paid any attention to those around him. He ran with his eyes focused on one thing, the finish line. Stride for stride, he glided on the track in a seemingly effortless manner, picking up speed each second and cruising to victory after victory. Horses wear blinders when they race on the track so they do not grow distracted by the other horses or jockeys riding by. Occasionally, a horse's blinder will come loose or it turns its head and catches a vision of all the others stampeding in close proximity. This ends horribly, as the horse panics and will often stop mid race bucking wildly in a frenzy.

Like a horse or a sprinter, each of us has a race to run and it is uniquely and specifically our own. In the race of life we are not to compare ourselves with others or stack our life up against other people's lives. We were all created and designed for a specific purpose. You and I have our own destiny to fulfill. The minute I try to do what you do or focus on trying to be like someone else is the minute I step out of my lane and start losing the race. The race is really against the clock and ourselves. We each have a set amount of time here to live and what we do with that time is our personal choice. Free will is a beautiful thing that God gifted us with. How we use it for the good in order to live out our specific calling is probably life's greatest challenge. Yet, in doing so we often yield life's highest reward.

Competition at its purest form is good. It pushes people to strive for greatness and become all they can be. What happens, though, is that we start looking over our shoulder and taking the blinders off. We look into the lane next to us and start going through the whirlwind of comparisons that leads to envy, thoughts of insufficiency, and jealousy. We are sometimes left feeling inadequate and try to be someone we are not.

As a little kid I remember going over to my cousin's house to play. I was a few years older than my cousin who was just a toddler at the time. He took the blocks that were out and started to push them around. Then he took one and went over to this other toy and attempted to jam the square block into a round hole. It wouldn't fit through. He kept trying over and over and started to cry. I went over to him and said, "It's okay, try this." I turned it around and showed him how to put the square block in the square hole and the round block into the circular hole.

We often fall into the trap of the blocks in our own lives and get shut out because we lose focus and try to jam things that do not belong. Do you not realize that you were fearfully and wonderfully made. There is nothing wrong with you. Your appearance, who you are at the core, is exactly what God intended it to be. God does not make mistakes and He designed you with all the right pieces to make a big splash in this world. Run your own race and stay true to who you are. If people have a problem with that so be it. God is pleased and you should be pleased as well. This "I am not good enough" mentality and comparing my life to yours is detrimental and causes great and unnecessary affliction. Each of us has unique gifts and talents we must utilize and celebrate. When we stay in our lane and run our own race, in time we discover or uncover who we truly are and what we were meant to do.

The life you have before you is one that you can change at any moment in time. But before that change happens, you must know who you are. You must take a long deep look at yourself in the mirror, understand to the core who this person is looking back at you, and believe that you are important. You have a purpose. Then and only then will you be comfortable in your own skin. Stop trying to please everyone. Stop being concerned so much about what other people think? Who cares. You cannot please everyone, nor should you try. If this is something you are worried about, I believe you aren't living right. Live your truth and do what you know and believe needs to be done. You should focus on the fact that we play and run our race for an audience of one. You do you. This will change your game and you will be able to focus your time, attention, and energy on things that matter. You will no longer waste time or fall into the trap of comparison or competing with the wrong thing in mind. The competition with yourself will drive you, and this will lead you to be the champion that you are and all that God created you to be.

When we run our own race in life it allows us to find our passion and utilize the unique gifts and talents that we have been blessed with. God has designed us and provided abilities that we can tap into in order to live out who we truly are, as well as providing a contribution to the world. Discovering the things you are good at and what you enjoy makes life so much more enjoyable. When we are able to marry our passion with our career that is ideal; however, having an organization, cause, nonprofit, or some other important and engaging venture to put time and energy into is vital. These endeavors add meaning and value to our own lives and allow us a platform to share our gifts with the world. I encourage you to think about what you really enjoy doing and to reflect on the talents that you have. Then look into how you may utilize those gifts and connect your passion with it to give back. You will be amazed at how fulfilling it will be and the amount of goodness that will transpire. After all, "God loves a cheerful giver." Who knows what kind of spark you will ignite in others in doing so. What I do know is that you will be happier and feel more whole having lived out your passion by sharing it with the world.

"Without self-discipline, success is impossible, period."

– Lou Holtz

CHAPTER 13: Discipline to Rise Above the Tide

"I don't stop when I am tired, I stop when I am finished. Stay hungry." -David Goggins

Left, left, left right left. Left, left, left right left. Marching to and fro, physical training, waking up in the wee hours of the morning. Being yelled at and having someone be up in your face. Anyone who has been through military training or is a college or pro athlete can understand the word discipline. Discipline is a word that makes many people cringe. They hate it because it is hard. Yet, it is probably the single most important characteristic that will help you win in life. Most people do not possess the mental fortitude to go all in all the time. Discipline is defined as control that is gained by requiring that rules or orders be obeyed and punishing bad behavior or a way of behaving that shows a willingness to obey rules or orders. Stay in line the commander shouted. Eyes forward and hands at your side. We will do this again and again until all of you get it right. There are no shortcuts here and there are no shortcuts in life. Shortcuts are the arch nemesis of discipline because when you take them, you literally cut short your potential in life. Stay hard and stay strong. "Sir, yes sir," the troops shouted. The next few months of your life will prepare you for everything that is to come. You will retrain your body and you will reshape your mind. All of the cadets understood that this was going to be rough because discipline infused to the highest level meant going against the grain and the habits that had been embedded for years.

Discipline is and should be applied to everything you do and be woven into the very fabric of your being. When it is and discipline is carried out to the fullest, winning is only a matter of time. The great Muhammad Ali took to the ring. Every time he laced them up, put on the trunks, and the gloves, the crowd went wild. They believed he would become yet again the heavyweight champion of the world. No one was better than Ali and his ability to "fly like a butterfly and sting like a bee," was something so many idolized. The heavyweight boxer would enter the ring and often in a matter of a couple minutes his arm would be raised, the match over. The referee would declare him the victor and the championship belt would be put around his waist. Why? Discipline!

In my life I learned discipline the hard way. As a toddler and little boy, I was a loose cannon. Timeout and sitting on "the step," the bottom of my parent's staircase became my new best friend. More like my arch nemesis. I had a fiery demeanor as a child and a ton of unharnessed energy. The rules were not something I liked to abide by. My parents had their hands full as I was constantly on the go. My little motor was relentless and if I didn't get my way, look out! My reputation was growing in the wrong direction. I was known for throwing the biggest temper tantrums so my parents had to put their foot down and make me toe the line. Legend has it that my dad who is 6'3" and a shade under 200 lbs had to practically sit on me to hold me down when I threw my fits. Discipline, I hated it. No! That was a word I uttered too many times for anyone to keep track of. So how did I become extremely disciplined by the age of eight? Well, it was exceptional and unceasing hard work by my mom and dad. They utilized systems that worked and after breaking me, the wild horse, I was a bit more tame.

By age five I was enrolled in Tae Kwon Do, a form of martial arts. I remember my first trip into Master Klee's Do Jang in Hudson. I had all sorts of nerves running through my little body. My mom had told me that I was going to like this new place because I got to be like the *Karate Kid*. How cool? You mean I get to go to a place three times a week where it is okay for me to punch, kick, and run around? I'm in! Little did I know, it was a bit more complex than that. The discipline that the next four years of martial arts trained me in was exactly what I needed. I learned self-control, respect, how to harness my energy at the right times, as well as the balance between force and peace. The yin and the yang became ingrained in me and part of my montra.

Week after week I soaked up knowledge from my Master including how to concentrate and control my body with precision to do minutes worth of patterned kicks, punches, and movements from memory. We counted in Korean as we did a strict regimen of jumping jacks, push-ups, and sit ups. And then there were my favorite activities of sparring with full pads, as well as breaking boards with our hands and feet. The metamorphosis that took place within me was worth every penny and the thousands of hours my parents sat watching me in the Do Jang. I traveled to tournaments where I competed with my team and as an individual. When I asked my parents many years later what they attributed my personal discipline to they said emphatically that it was Tae Kwon Do. It was something that I needed to keep me in line, on a strict routine, held accountable, and to learn intense commitment.

At a very young age I learned discipline and became a champion in martial arts. Here I am at age 8 after a big tournament.

If only discipline could be easy. See, nothing in life will be given to you. There are no handouts, nothing is free, and things don't come easy. Wrap your mind around this and stop living in a fantasy world. These are the facts. This is something that I emphasized when I taught middle school for all of those years. For some kids and for some people alike, it is a hard pill to swallow. I say this not to frustrate you, but to call a spade a spade. In fact it is better that life and the world is this way. Call me crazy, but think back to a time when you poured everything you had into something you desired. Recall the hours of time it took, the hard work, the effort, the energy that was expended. Think about how you felt when you finally achieved what you set out to accomplish. At last you did it! If someone were to just hand the trophy to you, would it really have mattered? No, there would have been no value in that at all. It is the grit, the long hours, and dedication to your craft that make one a champion. And that is why the saying goes, "To the victor goes the spoils."

As a basketball player and fan, one of my idols growing up, besides Michael Jordan, was the late Kobe Bryant. I would be remiss to say that I didn't think that life would have ended so abruptly and in such a devastating manner for one of the all time greats. What I admire most about Kobe was his discipline and willingness to work harder than anyone else to become the best he could be. So often as a kid I would turn on the game and watch Kobe take the court against many all star opponents. I admired how smooth his jump shot was, his handle of the basketball, and his amazing capacity to finish around the rim. Kobe was a lethal weapon on the court and was a pure scorer. You don't drop 81 points in a single NBA game and win five titles for the most historic franchise without being great. Greatness did not come automatically for Kobe. Sure, he was naturally athletic and gifted. Don't get me wrong, Kobe was not your average joe in any way shape or form. What I mean is that for years I did not realize the countless hours of hard work he put in before each game started, let alone years before which led him to become a legend.

Discipline was a quality that transformed Kobe Bryant's game, and something that he embodied and embraced to the maximum level. The average fan sees someone like the great #24 making millions of dollars as a pro athlete to show up, lace up the kicks, and play 48 minutes of basketball. Not a bad gig you say. What most people don't recognize or talk about is how players like Kobe got there. How he climbed the mountain and conquered Everest is by simply getting after it. Go hard or go home. Waking up at 4am, starting all the way back when he was in middle school, a young Kobe was hungry to be great. He would train and work on his shot for a couple hours before even heading off to school. Then, after class was over he got back at it. He would then put in another session after practice until dark and then do it all again on repeat. The training and working on his game was even more intense in the summertime, including four or five 2-3 hour sessions a day. This disciplined approach and intentionality is what led Kobe to become the "Black Mamba" and one of the greatest players to ever put on a uniform. The difference is that he carried this discipline and fire, which drove him to get into the NBA out of High School, throughout his entire career. NBA players came out talking about what they remember most about Kobe after he passed. The common theme was his fire that burned within him, his relentlessness, and his work ethic. Only a disciplined person shows up to the gym hours before anyone else is around to work on their game before the very game itself and then closes down the building at night, being the final to leave even after a win.

Making strides to become all you can be and live out your full potential does not come easy. If you want to be a champion in whatever you do and in life at large, you can, but commitment is key. All of this can occur and will happen if you want it to, but it boils down to one important concept, discipline. This virtue is not simply something that you are born with or just magically comes your way. Discipline is a key ingredient to a winning life that you develop over time. It stokes that fire on the inside and when it is tapped into seers a path to victory along a road of valor and high esteem. "At the time, all discipline seems a cause not for joy but for pain, yet later it brings the peaceful fruit of righteousness to those who are trained by it."

(Hebrews 12:11) Discipline is hard and is not pleasant. No one likes it, but it is extremely necessary to progress and to evolve. In order to reach our fullest potential we must have extreme discipline to elicit habits that shed our old selves and ways of thinking, doing, and being in order to become our new selves improved, better, stronger, and more focused.

Evidently, the hard things in life allow us to grow. You grow through what you go through! When life gets hard and things hit the fan, you can either make it or break it. The greatest, Muhammad Ali knows this to the maximum level. His training was brutal. He did things no one else was willing to do so He could be the best, so he could become the King of the Ring. Ali admitted, "I hated every minute of training, but I said, 'Don't quit, suffer now and live the rest of the life as a champion.'" So what is your take? How will you respond? Do you want it? Do you really want it because until you want it more than anything else, you will find excuses or ways around it. Procrastination robs people every day of getting things done. It is the enemy of focus and the thing that stops progress in its tracks. Taking ownership over what you do and how you approach life is crucial.

How you begin your day is imperative. It is what shapes your entire outlook and how your day will proceed. When the alarm clock rings the majority of people hit the snooze button numerous times struggling to get out of bed. It is as if they are stuck in quicksand and have been paralyzed by some wild force. When this occurs, motivation and progress already has taken a backseat. Don't be like the majority of people in our world, be different. If you desire a different result for yourself, you must start changing your habits. Habits are directly connected to discipline and routine. Make your day your boss!

One thing that I have implemented in my life to set the tone for my day each morning is called the "Heroic Minute." The Heroic Minute involves the initial 60 seconds of your day from the time your alarm clock rings to you starting your day. Instead of tapping the snooze button, open your eyes, shut off the alarm and thank God for your day. You are out of bed and your bed is made. You are ready to crush the day and get after it! The heroic minute was initiated by St. Josemaria, an all time go-getter and man who was daily working full throttle for the Kingdom of God. Sam Guzman had this to say about the Heroic Minute:

"The heroic minute. It is the time fixed, literally 60 seconds, for getting up. Without hesitation: a supernatural reflection and ... up! The heroic minute: here you have a mortification that strengthens your will and does no harm to your body. If, with God's help, you conquer yourself, you will be well ahead for the rest of the day. It's so discouraging to find oneself beaten at the first skirmish."

How we start our day in the first minute sets the precedent. Victory is either won or lost in the mentality that we set, the expectations that we implore for our lives. You snooze, you lose (pun fully intended). When we spring out of bed with energy and excitement understanding that there is unlimited potential for our day, our mind and body is ready to conquer. When we hit the snooze button and resort to laziness, our body and our mind already have faced one loss to begin the day. Do not submit to a habit of defeat, instead instill a habit of discipline and tenacity. Positive life habits and routine are what reshape the mind and form a new normal for us so we can push ourselves harder and be better than we ever were before.

Along with the heroic minute, I personally suggest you implement two more things to win each and every day. As a former collegiate athlete and as a fitness enthusiast it is instrumental for you and I to kill a workout to either start or complete our day. The body is directly connected to the mind. When we feel good and are healthy physically, we will have much greater mental strength and stamina. Like most things, it takes extraordinary discipline to leave the house early in the morning or come home later at night after a long day's work in order to get a solid gym session in to ensure your body stays fit and you look and feel great. You might not want to go, but push through it and get out there, there is no doubt you will feel better that you did. Embrace the challenge and do at least one thing every day that you don't want to do. This tactic will allow you to rewire your brain and build up stamina to establish greater discipline. Even on the worst of days, the gym session is a way for us to release our endorphins, relieve stress, and most of all know we accomplished something so good for our well being. Your time might be crunched, you say, then get a short run in, or crush some pushups and situps. The key is to get your body moving.

I am personally sick of people making excuses. You cannot and will not be a winner in life if you default and make excuses. Figure it out and get it done. The most common phrase is, "I do not have time." This is just a load of BS. You do not have time because you are not willing to make the time. It is not that important to you. If it was important, you would carve out the time to do it. Start evaluating your life and how you utilize the same 24 hours everyone on this planet has and use it for your good. What is more important than your health? If you have that, you have it all. Get up and get after it. Join a gym or fitness club. Become a member of an organization or group that will motivate you. Utilize the social media platforms that have free access to daily workouts. Whatever it is, like the Nike motto says, just do it!

Recently I logged onto Instagram Live for a killer workout with David Goggins. I should have realized that the man who wrote the best selling book *You Can't Hurt Me* and who was a Navy Seal for 17 years embodies the mentality to go hard or go home. After ten straight minutes of jumping jacks to warm up, yes, I said it, a warm up, we were ready to begin. The hour long highly intensive workout consisted of plyometric exercises utilizing one's own body weight to do a continuous series of pushups, jumping jacks, and flutter kicks. There was probably a total of two minutes of rest time combined in the entire hour workout. The next day and for three days after I could barely walk. However, during the workout I didn't want to stop. I desired to be like David who encouraged the 8,000 plus subscribers to the live workout to keep going. After working out avidly for over thirteen years and pushing myself really hard, it was one of the toughest workouts I had ever done. What I am getting at is if you don't challenge yourself, if you don't get after it, nothing will change. Put that ball in motion and give all you got and you will enter a metamorphosis in your body. The same can be true for your mind and your soul. When you emerge from that cacoon you will be spreading your wings and flying so high and so free. Starting is the hardest step, but don't forget it only takes one step to begin.

John Wooden in his book *My Personal Best*, emphasizes the importance of not making excuses. He discusses how excuses just set us back and get nothing accomplished. When we blame external factors it solves nothing. Growing up on a farm in the midwest, John's dad, Joshua Hughe Wooden, taught him what he called a "set of threes." Within that set of threes was the following, "Don't whine, don't complain, and don't make excuses." John discusses a time when he learned his lesson the hard way. He arrived at his basketball game in middle school and was ready to take the court. As he put on his uniform excited to help his team win the big rivalry game, he realized his sneakers had been forgotten. John pleaded with his coach to allow him to play. He said he was in a rush leaving the family farm and started to make excuses for this mishap. After sitting 32 minutes on the bench and watching his team take an agonizing loss, John understood fully that excuses do nothing and only taking responsibility by owning one's life was what mattered. Like basketball, life does not discriminate. You can excuse yourself or you can straight up own it. We will come back to this a little later, but for now it is important that we touch on keeping ourselves spiritually fit now that we have had a chance to work on our physical and mental strength.

Along with starting your day by ensuring you have proper physical health, is of course taking spiritual fitness seriously as well. Discipline each day is required to set time aside to spend it in prayer and solitude. It is critical to our inner well being to speak to God and let him know what is on our heart. Utilizing a daily devotional and reading the Word will totally shape your day for a win. When the soul is right and the body is healthy, you are going to absolutely annihilate the day. This one two punch will empower you and prepare you for everything and anything that you will encounter throughout your day.

Just think about it, your first hour and a half each day can accomplish a tremendous amount. You are rewiring your brain and through dedication and discipline you are changing your life in every major and important area. Your alarm clock rings, you got out of bed and are ready to take on the day. Your bed is made and you go downstairs for some breakfast. You spend some time in prayer and reading the Word and then you hit the gym to get moving. You already did so much and you haven't even headed to work yet. No matter what happens at your workplace, you have taken the initiative to set yourself up for success. As a result of your hardwork and dedication to both physical and spiritual fitness, you have become inwardly and outwardly stronger. You have the discipline within you and a routine that is rock solid, and will continue to progress over time. The foundation you have laid for your life is unshakable and something to tap into now in every area of your life. See, over time it will get a little easier and you will grow accustomed to this new norm that you set for yourself. Not to mention if you are a parent, a leader, or someone who aspires to inspire others, people will certainly notice when you crank up the discipline factor in your life.

Hard work beats talent, when talent doesn't work hard. We have all heard this saying before and know that it is true. No matter what you have going for you, it doesn't matter too much at all if you don't put it to good use. Conversely, when you seize the day and live by the motto, "Carpe Diem," you totally transform your life. For those of you out there who haven't started yet, today is the day. Today is your time to make changes in your life. Do not put off until tomorrow what you can and should do today. For those people out there who are already implementing this extreme discipline into their lives, keep it up. You know what it takes and you have seen the fruits of your labor. Ultimately, it is up to you. How you spend your time and what you do to start your day will be how the day will flow and go. If you want to be the best, you have to work the hardest. If you desire to become your personal best, make some changes, want it, plan for it, and execute. No one can stop you!

Stop making excuses. Find a way, no matter what it takes. Here I am pictured doing pull-ups off the roof in Santornini, Greece. Every day I make time to get a workout in. Making this a part of my daily routine for the past 14 years has trained me to be disciplined.

CHALLENGE #6: Attacking Discipline

Discipline is not our favorite word, nor something that comes easy. Your sixth challenge is to work on fostering discipline. This challenge is a week long one, so get ready. Look yourself in the mirror and be honest. What is one area of your life you really want to improve in? Is it being more productive with your day? Perhaps it is getting in better shape physically or eating more healthy. For others it might be taking a few minutes to pray or spend time with scripture. Whatever area you feel you need a kick in the butt in, today is the day to begin. Start with the Heroic Minute for the next seven days and then fully commit to the area you desire to improve in. I guarantee after this week comes to a close you will be feeling great and will desire to continue.

"If your actions inspire others to dream more, learn more, do more and become more, you are a leader."

-John Quincy Adams

CHAPTER 14: Extreme Leadership & Extreme Accountability

Twenty-two years later, I still remember game six of the 1998 NBA Finals. It was a sight that will always be etched into my memory, burned into my retinas because the greatest would strike again! Down three with forty seconds to go, Jordan brought the ball up the court and drove into the teeth of the defense. He laid the ball up and over his defender, kissing it off the glass. The home town fans in Utah were going crazy as they were thirty seconds away from tying up the series at three games apiece. The Jazz had possession and got the ball into Karl Malone, nicknamed the "mailman." He was known for delivering big in key situations at the end of the game, getting his team to Championship pedigree. Their go to player and Utah's leading scorer, Malone backed down the Bulls defender. With twenty seconds to go in the game, Michael came like a thief in the night, stealing the ball from Malone and regaining possession for Chicago. MJ dribbled the ball out on the left wing, behind the three point line. The clock continued to wind...12, 11, 10, 9...With 8 seconds left he made his move. Jordan was blanketed by the Jazz's best defender, Byron Russell. Michael took it hard to the right with two power dribbles and then crossed over hard to the left, making Russell fall in the process. MJ rose up from just behind the left elbow and drained the 17 foot jumper with just 5.2 seconds remaining. Ice water in his veins. The crowd in Salt Lake City was silenced, the GOAT had struck again. Chicago had taken an 87-86 lead, which they would not relinquish. After a desperation three was off the mark by Utah's John Stockten, the Bulls were again atop the basketball world. Jordan and Chicago had completed their second three peat, winning three consecutive titles. Michael was named the NBA Finals MVP for a 6th time and "The Shot" was forever cemented in basketball history. There was no argument that Jordan was truly the greatest to ever play the sport and possibly the most dominant athlete of all time.

Michael Jordan was a winner, but more than that, he was a leader. I along with millions of other kids who grew up in the 90s wanted to be "Like Mike!" The man who wore number 23 for Chicago for all those years pushed himself and his teammates harder than anyone could have imagined. His thirst for greatness transformed the game. MJ had a motor that would not stop and his will to win was unparalleled. Jordan was a coach on the floor. He directed traffic and led by example. He was always willing to do the little things, to step up in a big moment when his team needed him most. Michael was never shy of the big stage, but always embraced the challenge. He held himself and his team to the highest standards and was fully accountable. All of these years later it is more than stardome that I remember. It is Jordan's ability to lead, to produce winning team's, and to get the most out of those around him. He always made others better and because of that and his great ability to bring his team to the promised land, MJ has landed a spot in basketball immortality. And for that and all of his phenomenal leadership qualities, I still want to be "Like Mike."

I was the ultimate competitor and biggest basketball fan starting at a young age as a kid. I aspired to be great and had big shoes to fill.

Leadership is an indispensable characteristic that impacts everyone. No matter what area people work in or the realm they occupy their time with, we all are influenced by leadership. Many of you out there are already in some kind of leadership role, whether you know it or not. Some of you are junior leaders in your company, leading your various departments. While others are continuing to work their way up the ranks and lead winning teams in their industry as a president or CEO.

Whether it is in the workplace or outside of your career, you are all leaders in some capacity. For those of you who have a family, you are a leader in teaching and training your children. This is probably the most important area of leadership that will make the greatest impact and have such a strong influence, a spider web effect, on others for life. As the Proverb goes, "Train up a child in the way he should go: and when he is old, he will not depart from it." Do not discount the extreme value in being a leader as a parent. Your children want to be like you and the way you approach life will be instilled in them. Remember, the apple doesn't fall far from the tree. Do the best you can to ensure it's a good apple.

Some of you are spouses or have siblings. Others have nieces or nephews. These are all designated opportunities to lead. No matter who you are, where you are from, or what you do formally or informally, you can be a leader. We can either embrace this challenge and lead those around us in a positive manner or a negative one. Your life impacts others. Choose to have a highly enormous impact on everyone around you. Be a leader. Become the person in your family that is a rock that everyone may count on. You have what it takes, don't sell yourself short.

People in our inner and outer circles are always watching us. Many times they might not listen or even remember what we said, but they see how we act, they notice the way we react, and they are affected the most by the way we make them and others feel. Maya Angelou expressed this message of making people feel good who we come into contact with. A stranger or someone we love and know deeply may end up forgetting what we said to them or even did.

However, feelings tend to remain with us. We do not need to say much at all to be able to influence the people who connect with us in our lives. The best leaders are those who lead by example. Their very lives are a living sermon and pack a powerful punch as to how to approach life and how to win! Day in and day out these quiet leaders do everything with great enthusiasm and intensity. They put forth 100% in all that they do, which leads to winning results.

Leaders who show and lead by example are trusted, well equipped, and impressive because they are doers. When these leaders speak, people tend to listen. Their audiences know that their words are important because they are doers first. The verbiage that comes forth and the message they share is motivating to their teams because they back it all up with action. As we know, actions speak much louder than words. Anyone can talk. Frankly, too much talking takes place and not enough doing. I am a fan of the montra, "Don't talk about it, be about it." Get after it and show your team how by doing it first.

Another great quality of leadership is empowering others. One thing I have learned, after nearly two decades in the workforce, is that strong and powerful leaders are people who know their team and tap into the strengths of each member in order to make the unit better. This is a characteristic of leadership that is not very popular and is extremely undervalued. If more leaders took this approach, their teams would have increased levels of success and would even flourish. You have heard that we are only as strong as the weakest link of our team. This is true and it is a leader's obligation to train, enhance, and support the junior members of the team to build up their confidence, increase their competence, and accelerate their growth. Furthermore, the best and most powerful leaders know their teammates so well that they comprehend all they are capable of and what they are best at.

A team of players is made up of individuals who all have unique gifts and abilities that complement the squad. The best leaders are able to tap into each member of the team and provide them opportunities to lead various parts of the unit based on the task they are most skilled and well versed at. This is building leaders amongst your team members and empowers people. This approach enables the leader to build each person up and their team up simultaneously. Unfortunately, arrogance and the ego often get in the way of leaders. As a result it is commonplace that today's leaders take the avenue of simply telling people what to do, barking instructions from the top of the chain. It is unfortunate that they do not spend nearly the time they should participating on the ground level with their team. The old notion, "Do as I say, not as I do," is not getting it done. Not to mention this type of attitude is detrimental to those they are leading because they are not in tune with their team and are limiting the group's full potential. Leaders don't impose their will on those who are beneath them, instead they listen, devise a plan, explain the mission, and ultimately create an environment where all of the members of the team believe in the goal that is established. When the mission is fully understood and members of the organization perceive the "WHY" fully, this is game changing. With a leader who hits the ground running, is open to and looks for suggestions from junior leaders, and is willing to get in the trenches with the team, success will clearly follow.

The final quality of a noble leader is probably the most challenging, yet arguably the most influential of them all. The best leaders on the planet take extreme ownership and hold themselves accountable every day. Taking accountability for our actions is probably the most difficult and challenging thing that many of us are up against. It is not in our human nature to own up to mistakes, admit when we are wrong, or state that we have failed. This is humiliating and is something many people run and hide from. It is so much easier to pass the buck, place the blame, or point the finger at another person. When we are wrong, it is much less painful to make excuses and come up with reasons for why things did not go according to plan. The team failed because of X, Y, and Z. He or she did not do a job correctly, or this or that happened which set us back.

My first life lessons when it comes to accountability that I can remember go way back to when I was in primary school. For some reason I needed some big time schooling when it came to learning how to lose gracefully and with humility. Like most kids my age at seven years old at the time I did not like to lose; however, my passion for winning at all costs was on another level. During this year of my life I would learn some things the hard way, but it was what I needed most. On the playground toward the end of my first day of school I was in a heated game of two hand touch football. My squad was down by a score and we had the ball with only minutes to go. I took the snap, a blitz came my way and I was deliberately shoved in the mud. Enraged at my new clothes being completely covered in nasty filth, I quickly rose to my feet and started kicking and punching the big kid who had mercilessly tossed me into the mud puddle like a rag doll. Of course my parents found out, how could they not. I was covered from head to toe when I came home that day. They asked me what happened and I said, "Mike pushed me in the mud when we were playing football." Oh, I left out the part where I got up and was kicking and punching him, must have slipped my mind. My dad said, "You are not being honest. Tell me the truth. I know what happened." I need not say anything because they knew what I had done. I sat in the corner of my room thinking about my choices. A couple months later I was playing Monopoly with my older cousins at my grandma's house. This was one of our favorite games. I was set on winning and wanted to beat them so badly. After my turn and passing *GO*, I forgot to ask for my money. It was my cousin Kayla's turn and she rolled. I told them I needed the $200 for passing *GO*, which was a standard part in the game, but my turn had already run out. My cousin, Kristie, said, "Sorry, Dan. You missed your chance and lost out on the money. You will have to wait until next time when you pass it on your next time around the board." Fury rose up in me. How would I win now? In an angry state I grabbed the entire monopoly board and flipped it. All the pieces and money went flying as I stormed out of the room. And then there were sports. In Little league baseball I was a member of the Rockies team. I was 4-4 with a triple, two doubles, a single, and five runs batted in. Despite some spectacular plays at shortstop and doing all I could for my team we lost a nail biter, 10-9. I sat in the dugout and was pissed. I did not want to shake the hands of those Orioles players who snuck out a victory. Now our season was over and all summer I would have to hear about it. I refused to get in line until my mom came over and said, "If you don't get in line and shake their hands and be a good sport then no travel baseball for you." I got up and went through that line as fast as possible making no eye contact with anyone, a huge scowl on my face. I hated losing. Finally, mid summer I recall my dad taking me outside on the blacktop for some one on one. I was sure I could beat him. Clearly I had not learned my lesson of humility and being a good sport throughout this year so today would be the final straw. We were tied 9-9 and the ball was in my possession. Game was up to 11. I crossed over and took a shot and he annihilated it, blocking my shot into what seemed the next universe. If being stuffed like a Thanksgiving turkey wasn't enough, after collecting the ball he dropped back behind the three point line. My dad rose up, released the ball...nothing but net! Swish! The game was over. I guess I wasn't as good as I thought. He walked off the court after saying, "Good game kid."

Accountability was always hard for me as a kid until I learned how to lose, I swallowed my pride and was humble enough to accept defeat. I believe that it was in this particular year of my life, all of those years ago, and in countless moments since then that life has continued to teach me that excuses get you nowhere. Placing blame solves nothing. Being a poor sport or having too big of an ego to take the loss and bounce back is not acceptable. Those life lessons, that tough love I received as a kid shaped me at a young age to continue to work hard, give my all, and understand that when you lose or make mistakes you must take responsibility. In doing so I began to work even harder, be a better teammate, and grow into a true leader who is able and willing to take extreme accountability no matter how hard it might be.

How often do you hear a leader who comes out and takes extreme ownership of the entire situation? This is the quality that Jacko Willinick and Leif Babin expound upon in their dynamic book entitled *Extreme Ownership*. The premise of the text is all about owning every area of your life, especially with regard to leadership. We all could use work in the department of accountability. Taking ownership over our choices, our actions, decisions we make, and admitting our faults or wrong doings is hard. The importance of the leader doing so however, sets the precedent for the entire team and creates a culture of accountability which is critical for developing a winning team. Jacko and Leif, who lead winning teams on the battlefield for decades in the most treacherous and hazardous environments as Navy Seals, emphasized that effective leaders take the fall for the team as they are the ones responsible for teaching, informing, and guiding the unit. They are at the helm and must take full responsibility when things do not work out.

After admitting one's error, the impactful leader works hard with his or her team to make corrections and steer the ship in the right direction. Adjustments and solutions to problems are developed in order to go after it again and win. The noble leader is also one who does not take credit for the success of the team, but realizes that the very players who carried out the mission are the ones who deserve the recognition. The leader is not to take the spotlight, but instead to give that limelight to the team. When one leads in this manner, winning is accelerated. Those who are on the team will work harder and be more energized because they understand the leader has their back at all costs. Blame is not going around and the team members don't have to look over their shoulders worried that they will be "caught doing something wrong." A culture of accountability comes from the top and has a trickle down effect. Leaders cannot expect members of a unit to hold themselves and each other accountable if they, the leaders, do not demonstrate and model this to the highest level in every phase. Excuses must be cut out. The "I can't" or "it won't happen," must not exist in your mindset or vocabulary. Winning teams are built on positive regard and are motivated by the perspective that one elicits from the top, the very person who believes in them. Being humble and having the "always better, never best," approach is huge. We can all improve and there is always room to grow no matter how experienced we are. Together we can get better and in doing so we improve not only our individual selves, but the collective team.

Lastly, clear and consistent communication is a key to the dichotomy of effective leadership. When we are able to speak to those on our team in a way that they understand and break things down so it can be implemented, that will also change the game. The chain of command is huge according to Jacko and Leif who were chief commanders of their Seal teams. They understood this to the full, while serving in the Middle East during the Iraq War. The chain of command works both ways, up the chain and down to the bottom. People who are at the top must have an overall understanding and idea of what each unit is working towards and on, while those in each specific area are to inform the higher ups what they are doing and why they need what they need. This clear and concise communication on a regular basis is what these Seals argue is one more thing that sets everyone up to succeed and win. It eliminates assumptions and negates error by taking it out and devising a concrete plan. As the saying goes, "If you fail to plan, you plan to fail." A win happens when the communication occurs and everyone is on the same page understanding their roles in helping the team carry out the mission.

Overall, leadership boils down to accountability and leading by example. Each of us has the ability to lead in our own ways. Some of us will do so on a grand scale in our workplace or area of expertise, while others will take leadership roles in their families or life situations. We will get to the next level and lead others there by implementing these tactics and characteristics. Now it is your turn to go out there today and lead. The world needs you and you have a great amount to offer!

"Sometimes the most scenic roads in life are the detours that you didn't mean to take."

-Angela N. Blount

CHAPTER 15: Vamanos

We Go

Her cell phone buzzed, she just got a new text message. It was her friend. They had two extra tickets to the big concert at the stadium downtown. She was ecstatic! She told her boyfriend the great news. It was time to get ready and we would leave in a half hour. I couldn't go. I had so much to get done and besides it was the middle of the week. I didn't want to go to bed too late and be tired the next day. If I would have known a day or two ago maybe that would have been different. I explained this to my girlfriend and she grew visibly upset. "You don't do anything. Come on, just one time," she pleaded. A lump grew in my throat. I looked down. "Why does everything have to always be planned out?" she said with emphasis. She was right. Being spontaneous was certainly not my strong suit. I had always been a planner. Come to think of it though, this did sometimes limit me from having fun in life. What was the worst thing that would happen if I said to my girlfriend, yes for once. Not only would she be shocked, she certainly would be happy, and I probably would have a great time. Something dawned on me. It was time for me to stop being so robotic. I did not want to be "Mr. No Fun" anymore. This was my chance to begin redeeming myself.

After a two and half hour concert with some of our closest friends, we had an awesome time and made a great memory. I was glad that I had changed my mind after all. In life, we miss out on moments if our eyes aren't open and we are too focused or too serious. Sometimes you have to do what you normally wouldn't do to seize the moment. During these times of spontaneity a person opens up to great possibilities in life. You are able to experience fun at a whole new level and take advantage of the opportunities that come your way. Being spontaneous and flexible to seize the moment when it arrives out of left field will add more flavor and enjoyment to your everyday life. Not only is this beneficial to our personal lives, having an openness to what life brings our way will then flow organically into the professional realm of our existence as humans. In other words, by being spontaneous and willing to say, "yes," to different things that come to us, we will be able to more easily adapt to opportunities that come unexpectedly across the board in our lives. This will help us adjust a not miss out on the good that is merely one "yes" away. Let alone, the fun and excitement that life has to offer if our eyes are open to it.

My father-in-law is the very definition of Mr. spontaneous. I have never met another person in my existence who is more of a "yes" man to things, experiences, and people who come his way than Super Mike. It just so happens that my wife is the daughter of the guy who can do anything on a whim, accept an invite at a moment's notice, and fly by the seat of his pants. My wife and father-in-law are cut from the same mold when it comes to this adventurous side that I certainly lack in naturally. Both of them have led me to grow and be more spontaneous as the years have gone by. What I have learned from them is that not everything has to be planned and sometimes the best possible outcomes are never reached if we limit ourselves by cementing our whole life to a plan. There must be opportunities for childlike wonder, thrill, and enthusiasm that often comes and goes. We can either say yes and take the time to vere off for a little while or be rigid. Chances are, if we all added a little more spontaneity to our lives we would have more fun, do more exciting stuff that energizes us, and be more filled with life. The spontaneous puts the spunk in life and there is nothing wrong at all with a life that is truly lived!

Traveling the world is another avenue that I have grown to deeply enjoy. It might be cliche to say, but the world is your oyster. I would have never imagined that by age thirty I would have been to over 25 different countries and have visited 30 states. I mention this to you because exploration is a key ingredient that we can add to the mix of our lives that makes life much more enjoyable, in addition to helping shape us as people in the global world that is more intertwined than ever. Never has there been a trip I have been on when I didn't learn something new, or experience a unique place and what it has to offer. I have never regretted interacting with a different culture of beautiful people. Every time I go on a trip with those I love or even venture out on a solo trek somewhere, there is most often a big take away. Many of the best memories of my life are from traveling the globe with my family as I mentioned earlier in this book. Now I am blessed to be in a place in life where my wife and I prioritize saving so we can go on vacations and experience the world together. I have also chosen to get connected with different groups and organizations that I am passionate about, which have opened up new travels for me. I strongly urge you to do the same. Our planet is amazing!

We were not made to stay in a shoe box. Our feet were made to break out and explore, opening up new doors in new places throughout our lives. When we expand our own horizons by encountering people from so many diverse places we then have more acceptance, understanding and willingness to not stay stuck in our ways. Leaving the comfort zone of the shoe box or our home and stepping into environments, communities, and countries that most people only read about in history books or on a computer, is magical.

Save to explore because it will change you in a great way. Your love for others will increase based on what you experience and see. The people you meet will impact you profoundly. The depth of conversation and what you will learn from fellow human beings will blow your mind. And you will return home, bags in hand, truly believing and feeling that "there is no place like home." Yet, you will be eager to plan that next trip or take full advantage of the next opportunity that comes your way to get out there again and take on an adventure.

There is no time like now and this present moment to explore, live in a manner that is open to new adventures that come your way. Nothing in the future is guaranteed. As much of a planner as I am, and with how I like to schedule things out, the best time is to make it happen in the present. One of the most important lessons I have learned as I grow in some wisdom over the years is that you can always earn more money. We can always say, next time and have that mentality; however, time is the greatest gift and is extremely precious. Take advantage and do something every day that is new. Have fun and go out there and explore. Travel the world and make lasting memories you will be able to reminisce about when you grow old. Life is short, so enjoy every minute of it that you can. As we say in spanish, vamanos. We go!

CHALLENGE #7: Do something Spontaneous & Travel

Your challenge for today is two fold. First it is to become more spontaneous. I hope you have some fun with this one! Do something new that you haven't ever tried, go somewhere you have always wanted to go, or simply say "Yes" when someone asks you to do something. Spontaneity can really add flavor to our lives. The second part of our seventh challenge is to travel. Get out your calendar and set a date for you and your loved one, or you and a friend to explore a place you have never experienced. You will enjoy the anticipation of the future travels and it will be a memory you will have forever.

"Forgiveness is the fragrance that the violet sheds on the heel that has crushed it."

-Mark Twain

CHAPTER 16: Forgiveness

She was surrounded by a crowd of people. They were all staring her down. Her face grew beat red and she was full of tremendous guilt. Their eyes were piercing her very soul like a sharp blade slicing through butter. She knew what she had done was very wrong, yet there was nowhere to go. She could not hide. She was deeply sorry and she wanted forgiveness. No chance of that today, she certainly was fearing for her life. The crowd was bearing down on her, they were ruthless. She could feel their hot breath amidst the cool morning air, like a fire breathing dragon they glared at her with eyes that burned with indignation. The angry crowd picked up stones. There were murmurings among them. People clenched the rocks tighter and they were ready to hurl them at the girl. In a few seconds the stones would be unleashed in a fury. They were so quick to condemn her for her sin. She had committed adultery and she felt as if a massive "A" was being seared on her forehead.

Then all of a sudden, out of the blue came a man. He walked up to the crowd calmly and gently pushed his way through them. He maneuvered around the bystanders and approached the circle. The man saw all those gathered with the stones in their hands, grips tense, ready to hurl them at the girl. He witnessed the young girl in great fear, cringing and holding her hands over her head just seconds away from the rocks coming to strike her dead. The law and custom of their day was that one was to be stoned to death for a sin this severe. He opened the circle and walked to the center, taking a stand right next to the girl. The people in the crowd were wondering who this man was and what he was doing? What would happen next changed everything. The man looked around at all of the men and women who held stones ready to be thrown. He spoke, "He who is without sin, cast the first stone." One by one all you could hear were sighs. The great crowd groaned and the throng of people gathered around the circle dropped their stones. Thud, thud, thud. Each person began to walk away with their heads hanging and eyes fixated on the ground. A solemn mood set in as the accusers and those circled realized that they too were in need of forgiveness. Then the man spoke again. At this point it was only He and the young woman remaining, as everyone else had gone away. As people continued to walk farther and farther from the initial gathering spot, the girl slowly had the courage to pick up her head. She saw Jesus standing next to her and no one else anywhere in sight. She was in sheer disbelief. Just a moment ago she was surrounded by sharks ready for blood. At this point in time, she would have surely been dead. But, now by the grace of God, she was still alive and only one man was left, the Lord.

Jesus wrote on the ground and then straightened up and looked the girl in the eye and said, "Woman, where are they? Has no one condemned you?" She replied, "No one, sir." Then Jesus said, "Neither do I condemn you. Go, [and] from now on do not sin any more." (John 8:10-11) Can you imagine the feeling that welled up inside of that girl? Can you imagine the profound message this sent to the crowd who walked home ashamed of themselves that day? See forgiveness is something that we all need.

Life is hard and eventually we make mistakes. Human beings are fallen creatures and it is only a matter of time before we mess up. This is part of life. Therefore, it is essential that we learn how to be gracious with one another and forgive each other from the heart. No one is perfect and perfection is not even possible. As a result, we will do things we are not proud of and there are people we know who will wrong us. Of course, this is not something to take lightly. In no way is this an invitation to "do whatever you want" because you will be forgiven. Grace is not indispensable and forgiveness must not be taken for granted.

The story of the woman caught in adultery paints a very clear picture. We have all at one point or another been able to relate with each of the characters in the story. If we are truthful, even if we would not like to admit it, we have been those on the outskirts of that circle who are ready to hurl the stone at someone who has gravely wronged us or hurt someone that we dearly love. Human emotion and feelings cannot be hidden. It is okay to be mad, upset, and even angry. Nevertheless, what we do with those feelings and how we allow them to be manifested is the most important part of the equation. Certainly, nothing that the person did can be erased. Wrongs are permanent in nature and cannot be overridden. It would be nice if there were "do overs" in life. If we could easily and quickly take back the ill words we spoke that ignited a fire of fuery, or the wrong act we did that created a huge chasm and broke all walls of trust. This is not the case; however, we can choose to forgive and in doing so our forgiveness and mercy leads to love.

As much as we have been the ones ready to hurl the stone, we have also been the one in the middle of the circle. We have been the offender, he or she who is guilty of causing the pain, doing the wrong, and hurting or breaking the heart of another person. We feel horrible and wish we could go back and erase this terrible situation that we caused. We might even be ashamed of ourselves for the choices that we made. We are in need of forgiveness, a second chance. We need the opportunity to have another shot in order to do whatever we can to restore the relationship over time. It is this character who pleads and prays to be dealt with graciously.

Lastly, we have been like Jesus. Well, maybe not. Or maybe we have and can tap into this once again. He forgave the woman and did not condemn her. He did not judge or harbor hatred toward her in his heart. He did not talk down to her or make her feel any worse, for she knew full well the mistake she made and was sorry for her actions. See, inside you and inside me, we have the ability to love profoundly. We have the ability to forgive others their offenses, as our Lord forgives us. We can have mercy on people who do us wrong and sin against us, as they have mercy on us. And if they haven't had mercy yet, God has. Grace is necessary in life. It is something we all need and desire. It is the reason why Jesus said that he did not condemn the girl because no one cast a stone at her. It is the reason why our Lord taught us how to pray by accentuating the words in the *Our Father...* "and forgive us our trespasses, as we forgive those who trespass against us..."

We are all in need of forgiveness. This cannot be said enough. Backstabbing, revenge, the desire to make one pay. Unfortunately, this is the world we live in, a society which constantly wants to get even at all costs. Harboring resentment will eat you up on the inside. The hatred that is kept within will engulf and imprison your heart. Holding grudges will contain and trap you. Don't do it, it will eat you up. You will wear chains and until you forgive, those chains will not be broken. Without forgiveness you will be a slave to that situation, the bondage then cannot be broken. Hearts cannot be healed. Or you can walk the higher road, a path paved to righteousness. When Peter asked Jesus how many times he should forgive his brother he said, "I do not say to you seven times, but seventy times seven." In other words an infinite amount of times because over the course of a lifetime people are going to mess up. So do you go as far as to turn the other cheek? As for me, I hope to get there some day, but I will need some abundant grace to arrive at that kind of mercy.

Forgiveness is something that I have been the recipient of time and time again. As life progresses I am learning to forgive myself as well. I am grateful for forgiveness that I have witnessed and experienced while volunteering in prisons over the past year. Some of the greatest and most powerful stories of forgiveness have been shared with me at retreats in correctional facilities, as well as during our weekly prison bible study and faith sharing nights. Being an offender can leave you behind bars and even if we are not literally locked up, our heart can become just as cold as the steel that holds in an inmate. For most of us we can imprison ourselves at times with feelings of guilt and shame, regret and disappointment. For the guys I have spoken to and who have opened up fully to me, they are seeking forgiveness. Some of them have been forgiven by their offenders. They have shared with me discussing letters they have received or phone calls they have had with people in their family or community who they wronged. The men in prison have expressed that they "deserve every minute of the sentence they face behind bars and then some," as Drey put it. He even went as far as saying that without prison he would have been a lost soul and that jail saved his life. Being forgiven and granted another chance liberated him and many of his friends years before any of them would see the light of day outside of those prison walls. Bad and evil must never be condoned and accountability and justice are a must. However, mercy is a necessary ingredient when it comes to forgiveness. My challenge to you is to think about the worst thing you have ever done. Imagine if you or I were judged on this alone? We are not defined by a single event, nor should our lives or anyone's be for that matter. And yet, the crowd yelled all the louder, "Crucify Him, Crucify Him." The cross is heavy and a lack of forgiveness makes it even harder to bear. Hopefully we can all have some mercy, especially when one has a truly repentant heart.

In as much as we judge, and at times harbor this type of resentment that entraps us in our own misery, we can choose to let it go. When we do, we will become free. Holding on to it is detrimental to you and you will not be able to move forward. This type of mentality, this kind of radical forgiveness, is necessary toward others and maybe even more so toward ourselves. We are often our greatest critic, our toughest judge, and we do not easily forgive the wrongs that we commit. We come down hard on ourselves and then feel a sense of being unworthy. But the only thing that is unforgivable is your own unwillingness to forgive yourself and others. God's grace and mercy won the ultimate victory on the cross as we discussed before. The blood that was shed, washed away all of our sins. There is nothing that you have done or can do that will separate you from the mercy and love of the Lord. Keep this in the forefront of your mind. Like the one sheep who wanders from the fold, there is truly more celebration over that one that returns in Heaven than the 99 that are not in need of forgiveness. You are loved and God desires to mend and heal our brokenness because we are children of the most high. No matter what the circumstances are, no matter what sin or wrong you have committed, God can forgive you. You can be washed clean and be set free.

CHALLENGE #8: Time to Forgive

Forgiveness is another word we tend to cringe over when we hear it. This eighth challenge might be one of the hardest of all. I am challenging you to take some time and recall who or what in your life needs forgiveness. Maybe that person is even you. I hope that you can muster the courage to let go of the hurt and forgive, as it will lighten the load tremendously. Try your best to stop holding that grudge, drop the stone, and release it.

"Well done is better than well said."

-Benjamin Franklin

CHAPTER 17: The Little Things

She was in line waiting to enter the mess hall. As she stood at attention, her eyes were facing forward not looking around. She was ready to enter. Her stomach was rumbling after hours of physical training, she was ready to destroy her breakfast. A sergeant came down the line and peered at her left shoulder. She could feel his steely gaze and hot breath in her face. Then, like a loose cannon came an explosion of words that struck her hard. "Are you kidding me, recruit? Is that lint I see? What is wrong with you!" The recruit was in line and now more red than ever. She was embarrassed to the max and wished she could crawl up into a ball and hide from the world. Being reprimanded was bad enough, but being put on blast in front of her fellow recruits something she certainly would not live down. Welcome to the academy she thought. Only 25 more weeks of this crap. Why was I here anyway she thought. Why was the sergeant so uptight and getting on her for a piece of lint on her uniform. It doesn't seem right. People often tell us, "Don't sweat the small stuff," and yet she was getting reamed out for lint of all things.

When you pay attention to the little things and the fine details, it takes you to the next level. What the sergeant wanted to teach the recruits and the future member of the team that day, was to be aware of all the small things because when added up, they make a big difference. Not to mention, it was important for the recruits to be on the lookout for each other. Having one another's back with the small things will only prepare us for the future when we must take care of each other in the days to come in a greater manner.

The little things and finite details are crucial. Whether it be waking up and starting your day by making your bed, not leaving dishes in the sink before you leave for work, or keeping things tidy and organized, this is huge. All of these small things add up and make a large splash in our personal lives and the lives of others. When you have your mindset and focus on the things that matter it allows you to continue to do everything in your life with extreme purpose and intentionality. People who care about and take ownership over the small stuff create winning habits that spill over into all areas of their lives. When we neglect the little things and have an attitude of "well this doesn't really matter," that negative mindset and lack of intentionality can become commonplace. This is a slippery slope which often leads us to the point where we start sliding and compromising the bigger things. Before we know it, all areas and things that we do become haphazard at best.

He entered the clubhouse after walking off the 18th green smiling ear to ear. As the final putt was drained, he heard the crowd roar and gave his signature fist pump. He was on top of the golfing world again at Augusta National. The Green Jacket was his and wow did this victory taste even sweeter than many others. From out of the sport, he was back as the World's number one golfer. This was what he had worked so hard at. He had made a long, yet successful comeback. He finally rebounded and was the Tiger Woods of old. The fierce, determined, ultra focused, and tenacious competitor that strives for greatness and thirst for the win.

There are no mulligans in life. If you shank a shot in golf, you pay a price and are lucky if you can finish out the hole with a bogey. Golf is probably the hardest sport to master and it is extremely important to do all of the little things well. Every detail matters and then some. There is a 99.99% chance that you won't get a hole in one. That is okay; however, between the tee and the flag on the green where the cup lies is a ton of space. 500 plus yards of wide open greenery, littered with trees and sand bunkers that will eat up your ball in no time if you veer off course. Like golf, life doesn't happen and isn't lived just with one simple shot. Yet, it is played and mastered one shot at a time with great focus and concentration. What made Tiger Woods the greatest golfer of all time and the most dominant in the sport for over a decade was his ability and willingness to pay attention to the minute details. Shooting Par does not cut it when you are set on being the best in the world. So in order to light that scorecard up and be on top of the leader board by the end of the four rounds of play, one must be detail oriented. Each facet of the game is crucial from the initial tee shot to the fairway iron to the approach shot, short game, and then putting. If the club is off by a single degree in angle when it strikes the ball, it sets the golfer back and makes winning the hole that much more difficult.

Precision with everything so vital. If we would approach life like a champion golfer, things would be so different for us. What if every day you got up and were fixated on not just "parring" the day, but winning it by being extraordinary? What if we planned out what our day would look like in advance and then execute with precision? What if we consulted our "caddies" in life, the people we trusted and knew us best when facing a difficult shot so to speak, in order to choose the right club?. See life is very much like a round of golf. Whether you are just teeing off on hole number one and starting your round out, venturing through the front nine, or on the back nine approaching the clubhouse, each shot matters. In essence, each day matters and the little things add up as they become habits we will live by.

So how do you begin taking this new approach to really hone in on the details and care greatly about the little things? Well, it starts with one choice, one moment, one task, one job at a time. As we continue to maneuver throughout our day, when we go about whatever it is we are engaged in, whether small or big in nature through a lens of purpose and intentionality we will be more apt to maximize time. We will take care of the stuff that must get done and create ways of prioritizing through the use of making lists, goal sheets, and other metrics to help us stay focused throughout our day or week. Not only will this increase our productivity, but the quality of the work we do on the homefront, in addition to an increased sense of organization, will be apparent.

These new tendencies will then spill over into our work place, as we tackle our daily tasks at the job site. It is very difficult for people to merely flip on and off a switch when it comes to intentionality and paying heed to the small details of things. It is either something that we care about and is ingrained in us or it is not. Developing these winning habits is a choice. Doing so will not only increase the quality of our own lives, but the lives of those around us. Additionally, doing the little things well will allow us to grow professionally. People who are in management or who oversee us will notice that we took the time to pay attention to the details with great purpose. They will recognize that we went the extra mile and did something that most people would have overlooked or just moved over quickly. My great grandfather used to say, "Do what is right and do it right the first time." If you do not have time to do it now in the correct manner, then when will you ever have the time? He was so right. That is what you get from a five foot, 100% Italian man who built his masonry business from the ground up in Yonkers, NY shortly after the Great Depression. Hard work pays off.

Growing up, my dad was extremely meticulous. When I watched him work, he did everything with extreme discipline and purpose. My dad always took care of things and he certainly paid great attention to the details. As a kid during each season there were chores I helped my dad with. I would assist him with yard work and overall maintenance, as well as other tasks that involved manual labor. I learned a great amount from him through his purposeful and deliberate ways. I often wondered why my dad would do everything by hand. Whether it be sweeping the blacktop driveway after we mowed the lawn or clipped the grass on the edge of the sidewalks with hand trimmers, he did things in an old school manner. My dad told me that Jasons work hard. I gave him the nickname "Rickdiculous," for making my brother and me help him shovel our 800 foot long driveway after a snow storm. Why not just use a machine or take an easier and quicker approach toward these tasks? As the years went on, I realized that he very well could have taken an easier road. Nonetheless, my dad was continuing to pay attention to the small details and wanted to teach me to work hard. He did not forget about the little things and wouldn't allow me to either.

In life we all have things we must take care of on a regular basis in order to run our household and survive. But it is not good enough to merely get by. Instead, it should be in our mentality and placed in our DNA through this discipline and reshaping the way we approach things, to be our personal best. Something that stood out to me at a young age when I was reading the Bible was a passage from Colossians 3:23 which says, "Whatever you do, do your work heartily, as for the Lord rather than for men." This short, yet powerful passage, indicates that our approach toward life, the tasks we do, the job we get after each and every day is done not just for ourselves or our boss. It is done to give honor and glory to God. I take that as a personal challenge. It is not easy to be so dedicated to the small things all the time, but it pays off.

Whether you are a CEO of a Fortune 500 Company, a teacher, a public servant, a doctor, or a sanitation worker, the job you do doesn't matter as much as how you do it. The pride you take in your work is extremely important to shaping the trajectory of your own life and it speaks volumes to who you are as a person. How we go about our everyday job, where we spend upwards of 8-10 hours a day and over 40 hours a week is important. People at our workplace will notice how we do things and why we do things in a different manner.

St. Therese of Lisieux is someone who embodied this focus on the little things and doing everything with great intentionality. She was known for paying attention to the details. Therese was so humble and wanted everyone to learn from what she called the *Little Way*. She was especially doing her best to lead by example in how she approached daily life and the way she went about things to transfer her methods to others. Therese's approach has been of great interest to those who desire to be people who "walk the walk." The *Little Way* powerfully teaches us as humans to have both humility and gentleness, while being purposefully mindful in all that we do.

Each experience of our lives can teach us. Most of the time we are being taught in little ways through the everyday events that take place. Whether it was something good and pleasant or bad and heart wrenching, we can learn and we can grow. One learns from human connections, relationships, jobs, travels, mishaps, mistakes, the list goes on. Every time we get up and go, we experience something different. When we choose to look at the world through a new lens, we will be open to what the universe is trying to teach us. When we are humble enough to conceptualize and admit that we truly don't have all the answers, we will unplug the drain and knowledge will flow to and through us. When we take time to take in the beauty and intricacies that we are often missing, since we are constantly rushing around in a crazed hysteria, then we will quiet our minds and hearts enough to be open to receive new insights. We will embrace the little way and in doing so we will grow and glow from within because we took time to smell the roses. Stop, put things on pause, and just be. May the little way and stillness be embraced by you and by me as life offers up countless opportunities that can mold us and teach us to recognize the beauty that is right in front of our very eyes.

Growing up and now as an adult, I have come across a couple of people who absolutely have blown me away when it comes to the little things and the little way. Both of them happen to be amazing examples of people who pay attention to detail. One of them is my own mom and the other is my mother-in-law. What both of these incredible women have in common is their dedication and ability to pay attention to the lives of others. I am not just talking about what it takes to be a great mom and raise your kids, while wearing the thousand hats a mother must wear. They both have done and continue to do that. What I am speaking of is their purposeful use of time when it comes to making others feel significant and special. I have never met two people who are more in tune with writing and mailing out personalized cards for people's birthdays, holidays, bereavement, significant life events, anniversaries, and simple "thinking of you" notes. The time and energy they expound on this is impressive. What it says to the multitude of people who are the recipients of such acts of generosity is "you matter," and "you are loved." It amazes me that they do this on a regular, seemingly daily basis and preemptively before the event. The card is always in the mail and in the person's possession the day of or even a day or two beforehand. When we pay attention to the little things and do small things with intentionality, it makes a big difference in our world.

There is probably no greater example of someone who did

small things in great ways than Mother Teresa. Teresa of Calcutta dedicated her life to the poor. She showed up in their lives. Through her smile, bathing those who were ill, and sharing some bread and water, she made a monumental difference in the lives of those on the margins. Mother Teresa so beautifully and eloquently taught through her life and work with the poor the a powerful message, by doing small things with the greatest love poured out into each task. Life is full of finite details. When we stop to smell the roses and pay attention to the little things, we become more attuned with ourselves, our environment, and our human family. It betters our lives, helps to alleviate stress or frustration, and allows us to create a winning habit that enhances our quality of life as well as our relationships with others.

"You don't always need a plan. Sometimes you just need to breathe, trust, let go, and see what happens."

-Mandie Hale

CHAPTER 18: Step out of the Boat

"I can't change the direction of the wind, but I can adjust my sails to always reach my destination." -Jimmy Dean

The apostles were out on the boat trying to catch fish. Jesus had fallen asleep after a long day on the sea. The waves grew as the tide rose and the winds picked up. The sky began to darken and the calm water was totally gone. Worry started to set in as the boat began to take on water rocking up and down. Those fishing quickly brought in their nets and had to weather the storm. They frantically woke up the Lord who was sound asleep after a long day on the open water. The interesting thing is that Jesus did not simply calm the sea. He did indeed eventually do that, but He did much much more.

Before dispelling the storm and assuring them they would be okay, Jesus calls Peter out of the boat. He said to Peter, "Do not be afraid." He then tells Peter to step out onto the sea. Call me crazy, but people cannot walk on water. This was by no means a frozen lake. The Sea of Galilee during warm summer months was not your typical walk in the park. Peter hears the Lord as did the rest of the apostles. I can almost imagine them do a double take and murmur something to the effect of *Did you just hear what I heard?* Peter inevitably and faithfully listens and steps out of the boat. Very cautiously he starts walking on the water. But then he begins to doubt and his lack of faith and his anxiety take over. No bueno! Peter sinks and is submerged in the sea. The Lord has to rescue him. How many times in our lives are we filled with worry and anxiety for our future. There are so many things that we wrap our mind around and have great difficulty overcoming. Why? Haven't we made it this far? Haven't we faced storms before and been more than okay in the end?

What is more important here than anything is the act of getting out of the boat. I can only compare it to one thing, the scene that unfolded as Neil Armstrong and Buzz Aldrin took those monumental steps in 1969 on the moon. Imagine being the first human beings to make it to this far off region in Space, have the guts to get out of the safety of the spaceship, float along only attached by a small cord and plant your feet on the lunar surface. Truly that was, "... one small step for man, one giant leap for mankind."

Taking the first step or leap of faith into the water, so to speak, is super challenging. Personally, I commend Peter for going out onto those turbulent waters. Even though he did eventually sink, he did step out of the boat. All the others remained inside where it was safe and there was no risk at hand. When I walk along a dock or am at a marina it is a beautiful site to see so many boats. These vessels are all safe in the harbor. Even if a storm comes, they are tied up and sheltered in between the docks and the rocky coast. Although ships are safe at harbor, they were not made to stay put, they were made for sailing. In doing so, there is risk. Doctor Allen Hunt put it well when he said, "Becoming the best version of yourself will require courage and risk. A ship is safe as long as it sits in the harbor, but that's not what ships are made for. Your life will be comfortable as long as you remain where you are. Change and growth take courage."

As I think about my own struggle and experiences of taking that step out of the boat, numerous things come to mind all of which are pretty significant. What if I never would have asked her out on a date, we would not be married. What if I hadn't taken the chance to interview for that first job, or didn't put in for a final bid on the house. We can all go down the line and think of times in our past where we did get out of the boat and enter some shark infested waters. For me, if I did not take the risk or leap of faith, my life would have turned out much differently. Come to think of it, it is time to jump! Some of you out there need to set sail. You have been limiting yourselves too much and have played it safe for far too long. There is a voyage out on the open sea awaiting you. You may be captain of the ship and take off on an incredible journey. The first step is to get out of the boat or in this case jump into a new boat.

Change is scary. Not many people desire it. There are so many unknowns and great uncertainty that is tied to change; however, progress is not made unless we change. If we remain the same, we as human beings will lose our fire and become complacent. Complacency then leads to discontentment and before you know it, you are waking up wondering what you are doing with your life. For some people they never fully realize that until it is toward the end. They then have to face the fact that they wished they would have made some different changes years ago. As a result of not taking a risk or taking the initiative, they live with regret. What is worse than that, is dying with regrets.

This doesn't have to be you, but you do need to be bold and jump. I liken it to a small child who is going swimming in a pool. It is summer time and it is hot outside. Kids love to swim! They know the temperature of the water on the shallow end. They have their swimmies on and they are ready to plop into the pool. Things are safe because they can touch the bottom. They are okay and do not face danger, but there is so much more for them to experience. The child cannot help but see the diving board all the way down on the other end of the pool. They know that they cannot touch the bottom of the deep end. They look down there again. Some thoughts start stirring in their minds. They wonder. What would it be like to jump off that diving board into the deep end? They have never done that before. Children may be intimidated and even the thought causes fear to set in. Deep down inside where their fire is kindled, a boldness rises up inside of them and they get out of the pool. They start to walk down toward the other side of the patio. The cool wet concrete is felt beneath their little feet as their pace slows. They get closer to the deep end and hesitate. Is this a good idea? Maybe they should turn back. It is not too late.

Possibly tomorrow would be better. For some odd reason they keep going. They approach the ladder to the diving board. They look at it. They look down. A pit starts to form in their stomach. See, courage is not having no fear at all. Instead, courage is overcoming your fear and not allowing it to have power over you. It is defeating that fear in your life. The child takes their first step up the ladder. They climb a second rung and then reach the third. They are now at the top. They inch their way out onto the board and feel it starting to wobble. The child looks down and sees that it is much higher than they had anticipated. That pit in their stomach grows bigger and their heart sinks. They continue to edge their way toward the end of the board, hanging over the water that looms below. They can easily turn back and go the opposite direction or they can jump. This is their moment of truth. What will they decide? They have gone too far now. Today, they take the leap of faith. The child pushes down on the diving board and is catapulted into the air. SPLASH!! An explosion of water is thrown into the air. They have flown through the sky and have landed in the deep end. For a couple of seconds they are engulfed in water and then pop up gasping for air. They did it! Fear has been conquered. Wow, that was fun! The child swims quickly to the edge of the pool and skurries frantically toward the ladder for the next round. They repeat the process a little easier the next time and jump in again!

You and I are like the child. When we are in the boat or in the shallow end, we want to stay there because it is familiar. It is comfortable and it is safe. We know what to expect and we understand what the outcome will be. There is no risk. Yet, there is also no reward. There is so much potential on the other side. If we would only take that leap of faith and trust that we have what it takes inside. At that moment in time we will be launched into a new realm of possibility. After we get out of the boat, God will bless us for our faithfulness. When we say, "Yes," even when we do not know and have uncertainty, He will pave the way. Not only do we now have more internal strength by jumping, we possess the skills to get the new job done. We have taken on a new challenge and we will grow in our measure of faith because we took the quantum leap.

So what is the diving board moment you are facing right now? From what area of your life do you need to step out of the boat? How can you put a new song into play and a new sail into your life? Some of you out there are probably like me. You have been working in a career or doing something for a number of years and you are feeling like there still is more. You have been thinking about it and are no longer satisfied. Possibly happiness at your job place has flown the coop a long time ago and you are not content or feeling purposeful with where you are at. That is okay. Continue to pay attention to the signs and how you are feeling. Tap into what you desire, and listen. Eventually you will come to a realization. When you do it will be time to act. What you do with that intuition that you have, the conclusion you arrive at or prayer that is answered, is up to you. My hope is that you take the leap of faith. Be not afraid. The possibilities that are on the other end of that pool are incredible. You are about to make a huge splash! Now it is your time, just jump!

    Trust is one of the most difficult and challenging things for us as humans to do. Letting go, believing that it will all work out, while not knowing. This is tough to do on a micro level, let alone on a macro level. We all want to be in control and yet life has a way of shaping us, molding, us, refining us. Behind the wheel, grip held firm, we put the car in drive. Pressing down on the gas pedal it accelerates and we are off. We take a slight left turn and pull out of the driveway ready to take on another day. As we cruise along the highway, we are in complete control. This makes us feel good. We know where we are going and we know how long it will take for us to get there. Once in a while there will be something that might cause a delay, some extra traffic, and possibly an accident that holds things up. Nonetheless, we are behind the wheel and in the driver seat.

    Being in the driver seat of life is important. We go where we need to go and we arrive there because that is what we desire. Yet, driving alone actually limits us. There was a young girl, radiant with beauty. She grew up in a loving home with her parents Anne and Joachim. Her mom and dad were family oriented and they had a deep faith. The young girl was proficient in taking care of the household, as she learned to cook delicious meals, take care of domestic responsibilities, and she was a hard worker. She didn't have many cares at all. She was obedient and had a heart for the Lord. Her faithfulness really set her apart. Day by day passed and all was well for her and her family. She was thrilled to have met a handsome man in town one day, while she went to the market. Over the next months they grew closer and her parents were delighted that he would ask for her hand in marriage. The two became engaged and were so eager to get married and spend the rest of their lives together. They planned out the wedding and decided upon a place where they would eventually live after tying the knot. Life seemed to be perfect, they were in love, and most of all they were in complete control.

One day Mary realized that she was pregnant. She was going to have a baby. A new life would be entering the world. This was very troubling to her future husband. Both of them were very faith filled and traditional. How could this be? "Joseph, her husband {to be}, since he was a righteous man, yet unwilling to expose her to shame, decided to divorce her quietly. Such was his intention when, behold, the angel of the Lord appeared to him in a dream and said, 'Joseph, son of David, do not be afraid to take Mary your wife into your home. For it is through the holy Spirit that this child has been conceived in her. She will bear a son and you are to name him Jesus, because he will save his people from their sins.' All this took place to fulfill what the Lord had said through the prophet: 'Behold, the virgin shall be with child and bear a son, and they shall name him Emmanuel," which means "God is with us.' When Joseph awoke, he did as the angel of the Lord had commanded him and took his wife into his home. He had no relations with her until she bore a son, and he named him Jesus." (Matthew 1:19-25)

Mary had become pregnant by the Holy Spirit, as God had a plan for her to carry the Savior of the World! Imagine being just 14 years old, leading a fairly average life, and all of a sudden one day you are pregnant. Not to mention, you are approached by an Angel who tells you that inside of your womb is Jesus, the Messiah! Wow! Talk about an intense situation and something truly unimaginable. This situation seems to be one of the most overwhelming circumstances a young woman or any person for that matter could possibly be faced with. Trust. That was all that Mary could do. She was no longer in control of her life or her future. She was scared, nervous, questioning herself, unsure of life, and worried about her future. These are just a few of the emotions and feelings that probably crashed upon her like a tidal wave at the news of being pregnant.

Despite her faithfulness and piety, she was faced with a big unknown. Fear takes Superman and twists and turns him upside down. It robs him of all his strength and he is unrecognized. Fear often devours humans the way a hungry hyena tears a small animal to pieces after not having eaten for days. Yet, although she was certainly afraid and did not know how this would all turn out, Mary fully trusted the Lord. Trust is the cryptonite of fear, as it dissipates it slowly. Mary didn't allow fear to cripple her, but instead fell back on her great faith. She reflected on all of the things that were happening in her life, especially the unexplainable ones. In the very depth of her heart she believed that God had a plan that would work out for her life and the life of her future Son. Mary believed. Since she trusted that God would only have her best interest at heart, she could carry on. Her fear subsided because she overcame her anxiety. Mary's trust was so strong that she knew it would all work out.

What a profound example of trust. If a young girl can faithfully say, "Yes," to the most significant and exceptional call in the history of humanity, we can say *yes* too. What is critical for us to realize is that she was pondering and wondering how this could be. Mary was afraid and did not like being out of control. Her faith was tested in the biggest of ways. Meanwhile, she let go of the steering wheel and allowed God to drive. Taking the passenger seat and loosening our grip on the wheel is challenging. Still, there are times in life when we would probably not take the turn, go down the other road, or open the door without a little push. When we trust and take some steps out of our comfort zone, when we get out of the boat and jump into deep waters, then we grow. Comfortability results in stagnation and complacency. Living in fear leads to crippling us and self destruction. Somewhere in between is the uncomfortable area where we are challenged. During these times and moments of our lives we grow exponentially and the trajectory of our lives is shaped anew. So the next time you are feeling a call, you hear a message in your heart, or you know it is time to make the jump, do it. Just trust. Have faith. You will become stronger and God has something truly beautiful in store.

God's Thirst for Your Heart & the Heart of Others

While he was hanging on the cross bleeding and in agonizing pain, the crucified Jesus uttered five words in his final seconds. First, he said, "I thirst" and a moment later the Lord uttered, "It is finished." When it comes to trust, these first two words are extraordinarily powerful and they funnel themselves into what Christ's love is all about. The latter, which he spoke, tells us that Jesus did pay the ultimate price and gave himself up to conqueror death so that we might have life. More than anything else, our Lord wants us to trust him. He thirsts for our trust and for us to open our lives completely to him. As we have discussed, trust can be a really difficult thing. It involves risk, vulnerability, and uncertainty. Trust is not easy. However, God knows all of this and he wants us to trust him fully. When we trust in Jesus and understand that he thirsts for us and he thirsts for our hearts, then we will know how to draw closer to God and allow him to fully enter our lives. Jesus thirsts for our love and wants us to console his suffering heart because in doing so we are able to come to him wounded, sinful, imperfect and sorrowful as we are. We can approach the Lord just as we are and he will take us in whatever condition we arrive. At this moment, Christ can heal us, revive us, and give us his Sacred Heart, which is full of perfect love. When this happens and we trust the Lord with all aspects of our lives amidst our very pain, brokenness, hurt, or struggle; then we are healed and Jesus floods our souls with an ocean of mercy and grace. In his book Consoling the Heart of Jesus, Father Michael Gaitley said, "Mercy is love that feels compassion for those who suffer (heart) and reaches out to help them (arm)." In essence, Christ's outstretched arms on the cross are reaching out to us to come to him, as he welcomes us with his open arms so our hearts can be healed and we can be made whole again-holy.

The beautiful thing about this trust is that when we open up ourselves fully to God's love in our lives and allow him in, he will then open up himself to us through others in a beautiful way. After all, trust involves the firm belief in the reliability of someone. That someone is, not just anyone, namely it is the one, Jesus. He knows the crosses we face and we must trust that the Lord will help us carry them, he makes us stronger, solidifies our faith in him, and knows that he can use all things in our life for good. When we fully trust the Lord and thirst for him, as he thirsts for our hearts, then the mercy and grace that comes into our being will drive us to reach out to those in our world who are hurting. Having mercy on the Sacred Heart of Jesus and consoling the Lord through our deep trust and love for him, comes to full fruition by Christ living through us in our outreach to others. This is an important call of discipleship. By loving those around us, we are loving the Lord and consoling his heart. We console the suffering Christ by trusting God and by loving our fellow man. Jesus calls us to this love, as he did not come to be served, but to serve. So, we are invited by the Lord to reach out to the brokenhearted, poor, and needy in order to do the same. Jesus says in Matthew's Gospel toward the end of chapter 25, "Whatever you do for one of the least of my people, that you did unto me."

When we encounter Christ in the poor, we embrace our own poverty. We are filled with great love and are able to allow the love of Jesus to flow from us to those we meet. It is not enough to simply take a stand on an issue. We must stand with others and be one with them in what they face. When we do this, then the walls, the stigma, and the barriers are broken down. Human to human, life to life, a personal encounter cannot be replicated. But, it all involves trust. That trust is a bridge connecting two hearts and two souls. When we first trust Christ and he bridges that gap in our lives, then we can lovingly connect with others in a deep way. The depths of the human heart and connection with people is what life is all about. The love of Christ is here with us always and present in the little ones. The greatest poverty in the world is being unloved. It is a tremendous blessing to have the opportunity to share with others on this journey of life and meet people where they are, just like God does for us.

Love transforms all and Christ Jesus gives us all the fulfillment that lasts forever.

Having the opportunity to go and to spend time with people who are the downtrodden and outcasts of society is important. When we go and simply show up, blessings and immense light comes flooding in. The encounter that we have with the poor is something that is transformative. In doing so we console the heart of Jesus. We bring joy into the lives of those we meet and they lead us closer to the Lord, radiating the love of Christ to us. This intense experience is what continues to keep me going back to the places that nobody else wants to go. However, the fact is that the poor are all around us. They are in our workplaces, our communities, and in our schools. Poverty tends to mask itself behind various walls. There are all different forms of poverty albeit physical, spiritual, emotional, social, and financial. Whatever form of poverty someone faces, it can drain them, sucking the very life out of their inner being. When you and I show up in someone's life, we give them hope and these seeds germinate. There is no telling how much this renewed hope will do for a person or a community and in fact it is not up to us to decide. We plant the seeds and God causes the growth. As long as we remember that we are workers in His vineyard, we will stay connected to the vine. This will allow us to do God's work that He calls us to and our labor will bear much fruit.

Mexico City is a special place for me for so many reasons. Experiencing the beautiful people in one of the most economically challenged places in the world has touched my life in a profound way. I remember getting my invitation from a friend to join a group on a mission. A divine connection took place. I will touch more on this concept of the power of prayer and divine connections in the coming chapters because God is always working in our lives. When I learned where Hope of the Poor a nonprofit organization served the people on the streets of Mexico City and in the dump, I was touched. Going there and showing up was another story. So many people were supporters of my first mission and the one's I have served on since, as there is so much need in this place. And yet, we weren't focused on "doing" but the emphasis was about being. Craig Johring and Danny Leger, founders of Hope of the Poor, are two missionary disciples that have taught me so much over the years. They have shown me the love of Christ in and through the poor. As Jesus thirsts for our hearts, he wants us to bring his love to others to quench their thirsty hearts. Being present is a gift, a far more impactful one than most understand. Do not get me wrong, there was food, water and clothing brought with us, as these all served as a vehicle to allow us the opportunity to encounter the poor. However, the heart of the mission was to share Christ with others by spending time with our fellow brothers and sisters.

Think back to the ministry and times of Jesus. He certainly performed many miracles and all of these impressed the crowds. Giving sight to the blind, healing the lame, and raising the dead are all quite remarkable. It is not an everyday occurrence that these happenings transpire today. However, it is extremely important to recognize that as much as Jesus wanted to bring healing to people's lives, what he desired more was to draw them into his heart so that he could have an encounter and quench the thirst of their souls. Jesus was not merely a doctor for the ill, but one for the broken hearted and those who lacked faith. Recall the words of the Lord in Mark's Gospel, "...Those who are well do not need a physician, but the sick do. I did not come to call the righteous, but sinners."(Mark 2:17) This shows that physical healing was important to show the power of God, however the spiritual health is the most critical as that lasts forever and sustains the heart.

Jesus is in Mexico City. I saw and experienced the Lord face to face in the poor children on the streets and their distraught parents. Climbing down into a drainage ditch and seeing how those who are forgotten in society live, opened my eyes. I was blind, but now I was able to see. Jesus was in the little girl who jumped into my arms and clung onto me. He was present in the small boy who held my hand and wouldn't let go. The human need and desire to feel secure, to experience love, and comfort is extraordinarily tangible. No thing, no material good, not even food or water which sustains life, can replicate this need for intense love. Love is what the human heart and soul needs and that is what we shared in our ministry. Spending time with the homeless in the local parks and listening to their stories, hearing their testimonies, and connecting with them on a deeper level was truly beautiful. All the barriers, walls, and differences were erased. Skin color, socio economic status, level of education, language; none of that mattered. What mattered was the human heart connecting between myself and the person I was spending time with. What mattered was the warm hug, the holding of a tiny hand while walking on the street, and the kicking of a soccer ball to bring smiles to faces. I believe by bringing joy and love to the poor we truly are consoling the heart of Jesus. After a couple of days of street ministry in the parks, we took an hour or so bus ride to our next destination where Jesus spends much of his time south of the border. There was no seashore and there certainly was no crowd gathered in boats ready to hear the Lord, as so often happened in the Gospels. The stench was horrific driving into the city dump. Even from a couple miles out, the smell infiltrated the bus. As we got closer it looked as if this was a very mountainous area where we were approaching. Then, it dawned on me...The mountains I saw off to a distance were actually heaping piles of trash. Hundreds of feet tall with no end in sight, these garbage mounds were massive. For as far as the eyes could see, in every direction, was filthy, disgusting rubbish. Out of the enormous piles emerged the people who worked and lived there. How could this be? Who could withstand such horrific conditions? How was this allowed? It was very hard to wrap my mind around all of this. Even the thought of these conditions could be paralyzing. I quickly called to mind why we were there. As Craig of Hope of the Poor had reminded us on that bus ride in, we weren't at the dump to fix anything and certainly had not come to fix anyone. We were there to love and encounter Jesus face to face.

Walking up the mountains of trash to find other human beings, to be present, and hang out with the Lord in the poor was our main goal. And that is what we did. In doing so, I felt God's presence like I never felt him before. My heart was satisfied and my thirst was quenched. Looking into the brokenness of those people, I saw Christ staring back at me. The suffering crucified Christ gazed into my soul and my loving presence allowed him to be consoled. In many instances, all I could do was to look back at the people I was with and tell them through my eyes that I loved them. This made them smile. The loving gaze told each person on the other end everything their heart thirsted for, they were not forgotten. It said to them that God longs for them. It told them that they mattered and they were above all else greatly loved. We were there to love and to share in God's love. I felt the Lord and I believe that the children, women, and men I shared those afternoons with felt God's presence as well. Jesus lives in us and wants to work through us. The smiles I received, the hugs, the many "muchas gracias" uttered, and the hand shakes were all evidence that Christ was alive. In the midst of a mountain of trash, Jesus was present and his love reigned. After all where love is present, the Lord is there in our very midst.

A final place I felt the intense presence of Jesus was when I joined another organization called Baseball Miracles during one portion of a mission I made in Mexico City in January of 2020. Having the privilege and opportunity to team up with MLB pros, coaches, and staff, as well as other volunteers part of this dynamic nonprofit to provide a dream day for kids at the city dump was spectacular. Over 150 kids and their families came out for a one day baseball clinic right there on the edge of the city dump as we transformed a massive patch of dirt into baseball heaven. Once again, love conquered all. The kids were provided and fitted with new baseball gloves, t-shirts, baseball cards, a backpack, and a good old fashioned ball-park frank lunch. We taught them the ins and outs of the game including hitting, base running, fielding ground balls and catching pop flies, as well as the mechanics of throwing. I have never seen so many kids so happy, as they smiled ear to ear. That day in particular changed my life and led me to become a member of the Baseball Miracles team! This nonprofit organization travels the globe bringing hope to underserved communities through the game of baseball and the love shared with the kids on the diamond. The human connection felt that day broke down all barriers yet again and it allowed these children to simply be kids having fun!

My hope is that you too will seek out opportunities to encounter Christ in the poor. Jesus thirsts for you with all his heart. He desires for you to trust him above all else. He will quench your thirsty heart and give you his heart for others. You will then be able to take a step out of your comfort zone and reach out to people in need in a new way. Your love will burn so red hot that it will shine like the brightest of lights amidst the most tragic situations, poorest of places, and the most hopeless of people. Remember, the poor are all around you. Invite someone into your conversation, take a few minutes out of your day to be present, and love someone like Jesus did. Your willingness to love and show up in the lives of another person will sprinkle light and make this world a better place. Your heart will grow and be so full because in loving you are consoling the heart of Christ. In loving you are bringing the Lord to others and they are receiving Jesus, who will quench their thirst. It is interesting that when Jesus met the woman at the well, over 2,000 years ago, neither of them left that day having taken even a sip of water. The Lord knew that she was hurting, having had five husbands and yet she still felt so empty and alone. Christ went to her and said, "Everyone who drinks this water will be thirsty again; but whoever drinks the water I shall give will never thirst; the water I shall give will become in him a spring of water welling up to eternal life." (John 4:13-14) The woman wanted and needed life giving water and that is what she received that day. Her spiritual thirst was so great, yet in one encounter our Lord quenched the dryness in her soul. When we love others and allow the love of Christ to flow through us to people we encounter, they too will receive life giving water. In doing so, there is no doubt that those we love will feel whole and we will feel whole as well. This is when we become holy. We are called to be saints and we can change the world one person, one encounter, and one relationship at a time. Never forget that God thirsts for you. In loving others, the Lord not only quenches the thirst of us, but the thirst of those we serve. Trust the Lord completely and see where you are taken, as his mercy and love are endless. Just say yes and Jesus will flood your soul.

"Our greatest ability as humans is not to change the world; but to change ourselves."

-Mahatma Gandhi

CHAPTER 19: Wild & Free

Life has an interesting way of throwing things at us. It presents opportunities and we are called to things that we never could have imagined. What we must know is that not only is this okay, it is much better than okay. It is actually hidden beauty. Without being stretched, without getting out of our comfort zone, we would be limited. Some of us are living life like a circus animal. We go through the motions of daily life. We wake up, go to work, come home and then do it all again on repeat. Routine is a good thing, don't get me wrong. Even so, living life in "zombie mode" on autopilot is detrimental to say the least. For a good portion of people out there, life goes by without much thought, not much excitement, and it is what it is. What kind of life is that? You get one life, it is time to uncage yourself.

Growing up, along with family vacations, my parents did a great job of providing experiences for my brother and I to see new things. Ringling Brothers Circus would be coming to town. At the time, my dad worked up in Albany near the Capital and heard that the big tent and show was headed for the Pepsi Arena. My brother and I like most little kids liked animals, so my parents figured that taking us to the circus would be some good family fun. My brother was most excited to see his favorite animal, the elephant, while I most wanted to witness a lion leaping through a burning ring. I had only seen commercials of this on TV before and couldn't believe we were actually going! Colorful clowns were juggling atop unicycles, performers were swinging high in the air doing crazy flips and twists on the trapeze, and the sweet smell of cotton candy filled the arena. Showtime was well underway and we had a prime seat, indulging in the magic and fantastic arrangements that wooed thousands, leaving them on the edge of their seat. At the time I did not think about what circus life would be like for those performers who were constantly on the go, much less the wild animals they forced to execute dangerous tricks. This was exploitation at its finest.

In the circus the lion had two shows a day. It was sitting in its cage with its head slumped and resting on its front paws. Powell's eyes were glazed over and he was staring into the distance. From where his cage was located, all he could really see was part of the sidewall of the arena and the back entrance to the stage. This was the only life that Powell had ever known. He was born into circus life as his mom, Prunella, had been a great performer and she bred other baby lion cubs. The smell of cotton candy, the roar of the crowd, and spending countless hours behind steel bars was all he knew.

Day after day, Powell would sit there in his cage, locked up. He would be let out a few minutes before *Show Time* to rehearse the act that he and his trainer would perform in front of an audience of thousands. Then after a couple minutes on the grand stage, Powell would receive his reward, a juicy steak. He would chomp down and furiously endulge until all that was left was the bone. After his post circus meal, Powell would put his head down and fall asleep behind the bars once again. On non event days, Powell was let out of the cage to practice for a half hour or so and get a little exercise after the routine. Every time he would do a trick, jump through a flaming hoop, or dance on a ball, he received a reward. Then the time was up and he went back behind the cold steel bars, the prison, his dark fate.

Powell never had the chance to be a lion. He looked like a lion, walked like a lion, and even could roar like a lion, but he was not a lion. For years and years his fate had been to travel in the circus, put on a show, and then be shoved back into a small confined cage. Oh what a life outside of the Big Top Tent that would have been. Oh what it would be to run wild and free! Out on the Savanna in Africa, with the rising of the sun, everyday springs forth new life. The lion wakes up to the hot rays beating down on his skin and has miles and miles of open grasslands before him to go out on the hunt to catch today's feast. It is untamed, wild, and free! The lion embraces the wilderness and has limitless potential. The freedom and excitement to prowl about searching for a gazelle or antelope excites him. Powell dreams of such a life, one where he can go out on the hunt. A life full of natural beauty, using his powerful legs to run at full speed to track down the prey. A life where he is able to utilize his sharp claws and robust jaws to chomp down on the gazelle, while using his sharp teeth that shred it to pieces like a razor blade. Powell is not living wild and he certainly is the furthest from freedom. He lets out a fierce and resounding roar. If he did this in the wild, the rest of the jungle would surely know that he is king! The pride would follow him and his lead. All the creatures in the kingdom would have the utmost respect and reverence for Powell who is atop the food chain and living life to the fullest. Powell is no longer merely alive, going through the motions of the day. He is not fine or okay anymore. Powell is a lion through and through, a force to be reckoned with, a beast!

"I'm fine," she said. "I'm okay," he replied. No! You are not fine and you are not okay. Stop limiting yourself and stop pretending. Confined to a box, confined to labels or what society tells you that you should be. Mediocrity, average, just drifting by. This is not the life you and I are deemed to live. This is not who you are at the core. Wake up! As author Glennon Doyle in her book *Untamed* explains, "I'm fine means that you are half dead." Stop going around pretending that things are to your liking. There is so much more. We often cage ourselves. We have a tendency to be like Powell. In our inner being is a beast, there is a lion inside. The very soul at its epicenter has this fierce, brave, and beautiful tenacity that is bottled up and pressed down. It is time to unleash the beast. Uncage the animal inside. It is time to thrive.

There are enough average people out there. Plenty of us have been floating and drifting for long enough. Take life by the horns. Chase down your destiny! Grab the gazelle by the neck and shred it to pieces. You are a beast and the beast inside of you must be released. Your life has too much potential to sit there and not go after your goals, not go after your dreams, not become the best and fullest version of yourself. Stop settling and stop allowing the world, the people around you, and social norms to throw you in a cage and lock the door. Bust out of it. Find a way today, to set a new path and blaze a new trail for your life. You only get one chance, one opportunity, one shot. You can choose to remain in the cage and be confined behind bars doing what you have always done. You can continue to be just a shell of your truest and purest self or you can be wild and free.

Become a wild beast who prowls around and seek out your desired prey. This transformation won't be easy, but when it happens, you, the lion, will know what it wants and will chase it down. You will devour your hunger for life and stoke the fire burning within. It will more than satisfy the beast that exists inside of you. Make a decision. See, beasts go into beast mode every day. There is a switch that turns on in the morning when they rise and are ready to grind. They do not take no for an answer and the beast is constantly on the hunt. Take some time to gather yourself so that you can release the inner beast. This is your year, your time to put aside the things that have been confining you, caging you, and holding you back. Imagine your life now. Think about Powell and be the lion that roars askKing of the jungle and king of your life. Claim your crown. You have what it takes, run wild, and run free!

Glennon Doyle threw a knockout punch when explaining in the most powerful way how we can live our best life and become who we are meant to be. In her book *Untamed,* she elaborates on the crucial notion of not containing ourselves or being confined to anything. If we are to truly live freely we must untame and uncage our minds, our bodies, our ideas, our expectations, and our hearts. Glennon has lived by the idea of busting out and truly living! The *New York Times* best selling author had this to say, articulating the evolving nature and fierce beauty that exists within us, as we are hungering for more:

"The memos I've written for myself or neither right nor wrong; they are just mine. They're written in the sand so that I can revise them whenever I feel, know, imagine a truer, more beautiful idea for myself. I'll be revising them until I take my last breath. I am a human being, meant to be in perpetual becoming. If I am living bravely, my entire life will become 1 million deaths and rebirths. My goal is not to remain the same but to live in such a way that each day, year, moment, relationship, conversation, and crisis is the material I use to become a true or, more beautiful version of myself. The goal is to surrender, constantly, who I just was in order to become who this next moment calls me to be. I will not hold onto a single existing idea, opinion, identity, story, I am a human being, meant to be in perpetual becoming. If I am living bravely, my entire life will become 1 million deaths and rebirths. My goal is not to remain the same but to live in such a way that each day, year, moment, relationship, conversation, and crisis is the material used to become a true, more beautiful version of myself. The goal is to surrender, constantly, who I just was in order to become who this next moment calls me to be. I will not hold onto a single existing idea, opinion, identity, story, or relationship that keeps me from emerging new. I cannot hold too tightly to any riverbank. I must let go of the shore in order to travel deeper and see farther. Again and again and then again. Until the final death and rebirth. Right up until then." (page 77, Untamed)

"If you look at what you have in life, you'll always have more."

-Oprah Winfrey

CHAPTER 20: Gracias

Thank You

Pharell Williams quickly took the world by storm with his infamous song that made him an instant celebrity. In less than four minutes of singing and dancing, the lyrics and music video produced by the young prodigy was listened to by millions around the world back in 2014 and still is to this day. His song entitled *HAPPY* captivated the music industry and put him on the map. The title of his song is exactly what we all desire, namely to be happy. So what makes someone happy? Or as Pharell sang in the hit song of the year, what makes someone "feel like a room without a roof"? How can we live out this anthem and increase our own happiness and the level of happiness in those around us? There have been numerous studies, books written, and even a class is now offered by Yale University on this important and age-old topic. What is happiness and what makes someone genuinely happy? It is time for us to clap along and allow happiness to be our truth.

Every human being desires to be happy. We want to feel good on the inside and be immersed with positivity. We all crave things that make us smile and give us a type of euphoria. It is important to be happy for our own physical, mental, emotional, and spiritual well being. Happiness is something that is contagious as well. When we are happy the people in our family, our friends, and colleagues are drawn in and come closer to us. Happiness is attractive. So how can we become happier? What is it that we can do every day to control and impact our own happiness, as well as radiate this energetic state to others because they deserve to be happy too.

First of all, happiness in its deepest and purest sense for me is closer to joy. When I think of happiness at its core it is more aligned to what makes one joyful. I say this because happiness on a surface level is pretty fleeting. Take shopping for example. When I go to the mall and buy a new pair of sneakers or the latest electronics, I am "happy" for a little while. After a few days or maybe even a number of hours, that feeling goes away and I am searching for something else to fill its place. I desire to plug in another thing, event, or experience to make me "happier." Happiness as it relates to the sustained inner feeling of goodness or completeness, being whole and filled up, is joy. Joy is lasting and it is not short-lived. Joy or happiness in this regard, is an inner sense of gratification and peace, where that goodness does not wane away, but remains. This type of happiness is something we as humans really desire and need.

One way to be filled with that true and lasting happiness or joy, whatever you would like to name or call it, is gratitude. Gratitude is life changing. The energy and positivity that comes to us when we elicit an attitude of daily gratitude is tremendous. This is something each of us can do in a small way every day to improve our overall well being and level of pure and lasting happiness. It is said that the most happy people are typically the most grateful people. That makes sense. When we take time to look back and reflect on all that we have been blessed with and all of the good and positive things in our lives, we will smile. A spring of joy will well up within us and a feeling of goodness that is almost unexplainable will take place.

Although I cannot speak for everyone, most of us who are able to read this book have at least been educated in some way and are doing well enough to get their hands on this piece of literature. Whether we are in the middle class of society, at the top level of the wealthy realm, or another area when it comes to financial stability, we all have things to be grateful for. I challenge you to take five minutes right now to jot down all of the positive things you have going for you in your life. Simply list all of the people, places, experiences, and things that you are thankful for and it will surely surprise you. Most of the time there tends to be a whole lot more on that list than we might have thought was the case. This is so good because there is a lot for us all to be grateful for.

Over a decade ago, I was riding the bus in the city of Syracuse going from my dorm room at Le Moyne College to the Samaritan Center, the local soup kitchen. I had taken the bus weekly to go and volunteer during the mornings to lend a hand and serve the poor. Every day, some new faces and some familiar ones entered Bus #39 enroute to downtown. On one particular morning in the early spring, snow was melting from the ground and the birds were chirping as I walked toward the bus stop. I got onto the bus and sat down. Most days it was quiet in the early morning during that bus ride to downtown; however, on this particular morning the elderly woman who sat next to me greeted me with a big smile. She introduced herself. Her name was Florence.

Based on appearance, I guessed that Florence was in her 60s. She asked me what I, a college student, was doing up so early, let alone on a city bus headed downtown. Florence was surprised to hear where I was going and thought that was really nice. She must have sensed that I had some level of faith through the activity I was set to do and asked if I could pray for her. I said of course I would. What she shared next was quite alarming. It is not every day that someone that you just meet for the first time shares with you something very deep during your initial encounter. Florence poured out her heart on that CDTA ride that morning and told me that her grandson was killed the week before by a bus that hit him and left him dead instantly. I was shell shocked. How could this woman be smiling when she spoke to me and greeted me when I entered the bus? How could she still have a positive attitude and demeanor after losing her seven year old grandson? The pride and joy of her life was mercilessly taken from her.

I was speechless. Florence then said, "It is a great day to be alive. My feet hit the floor this morning and God has blessed me." Next, she went on to tell me that every day was a blessing. Florence's life montra I would learn was, "Every day when I wake up and my feet hit the floor is a good day. God continues to bless me." There is a reason why I remember those words she spoke to me all those years ago. Later on, I learned that Florence was a college janitor in the women's dorm of my campus in St. Mary's Hall. It is because of her attitude and her gratitude, in which I was awoken and brought me to the next level. From that day on, after meeting Florence and having that encounter, I realized that I needed to be more grateful.

I vowed to thank God every day when my eyes opened in the morning and my feet hit the floor because life is a precious gift and must never be taken for granted. I too, had so much happiness to be filled with and it was my job to also share that with others to brighten their day.

We all have things to be grateful for. From the very air and breath that fills our lungs to the beautiful people that surround us in our family. Some of you are thinking, *this guy doesn't know my relatives*. Okay, so besides that crazy uncle or strange great aunt, you know what I mean. The jobs that we hold, even if they are not the most exciting, allow us to afford a place to live and to have food on our table. Our work gives us purpose and a place of belonging on a weekly basis. We have so many possessions that we can be grateful for as well. What is more though are the relationships we have with those in our inner circle, our spouse, siblings, parents, grandparents, cousins, aunts, uncles, and children. We are thankful for the deep friendships we have fostered over the years with people who know us to the core. A spring of gratitude wells up from thinking about the people who know us in a deep and profound way. People we can and do tell everything to, those we trust with every fiber of our being.

Then there are life experiences. Whether that be opportunities to engage in activities that we enjoy albeit sports, hobbies, clubs, and organizations or times we were able to travel. Every time we have a chance to do something new and encounter a place or a group of people we have never experienced before it allows us to expand our horizons and grow. For this we should be grateful.

Health is probably the most precious and finite gift. There are many things we can do to improve and foster good health. That is why I chose to exercise everyday and eat a plant based diet. Just some food for thought, no pun intended. And yet there are so many things out of our control. When we have our health we must be grateful because this allows us to excel and lead the life we desire to its fullest extent. Gratitude is one word that can radically and exponentially change the game for us in our lives.

Finally, there is our faith. Being thankful for the faith we have been blessed with and God's love and promise to take care of us in this world and in the world to come is a gift for everyone to receive. Mother Teresa mentioned that the word JOY is really an acronym for how we should live. She said it stood for Jesus, Others, Yourself. Mother Teresa expressed that when we choose to live life in this order, we will be most happy. That doesn't mean we have to pour from an empty cup or sacrifice everything at the expense of our very selves. It is just a small reminder that happiness comes from within and we "reap what we sow." The love of God and His blessings that reign down on us are beautiful. Even the times when we struggled, and suffered, and barely were able to get by, we made it somehow and in some way. We can be grateful that we overcame those dark times and tragic moments. Most likely there was someone who helped us, something that came to us when we needed it most, that propelled us forward. Even if we had to do it all alone and we had no one by our side, we can be grateful that the situation is now over or at least has improved. We are still alive and there is hope for our future.

Some of us have this attitude of gratitude already, while others, like me, might struggle from time to time. Moments in our lives like my encounter with Florence often put things in perspective and help us to re-center ourselves and our appreciation of things. As I mentioned before, I have had many opportunities to serve the poor throughout the world. When I encounter people on the streets and in the dump in Mexico City or when I was in Kenya, Africa in the slums it rattled my inner being. My very soul was shaken. These large encounters and noteworthy experiences certainly upped my level of gratitude. What I have learned is that there is great power in giving and eternal reward. In chapter 25 of Matthew's Gospel, verse 40 powerfully states, "And the king will say to them in reply, 'Amen, I say to you, whatever you did for one of these least brothers of mine, you did for me'." Whatever you did for the least. It is beautiful to come face to face with Christ in the poor, it will change your life and the gratitude and love inside of you will be launched like a rocket into a new stratosphere. You and I were made for greatness and part of that is a mission to love on others, especially those who need it most, namely the deemed unloveable on the margins of society.

Going off to far away lands and having exposure with radical destitution will help you learn gratitude, which then results in increased happiness. However, the poor are all around you and there are other ways to ignite that flame of gratitude, service, and love. Personally, one thing, I recommend, that can truly change your life in terms of gratitude and happiness are the Spiritual Exercises and the *Examen* by St. Ignatius of Loyola. In the *Examen*, at day's end, you take five minutes to reflect on your day. You think back prayerfully to the times you felt God's presence, something good came your way, and you experienced love. This provides time and space for us to be grateful for the small moments that occured in the busy day and recall happiness. Next, we *Examen* or reflect on the times when perhaps we missed the boat so to speak and did not receive or emulate love or appreciation in our day. We do this to grow and become better, more well in tune for tomorrow. The *Examen* is an exercise that can change your life. As you go through this reflection on a daily basis, not only will your own level of happiness and gratitude increase, but you will begin noticing the goodness and positive events around you; namely, where love is felt, expressed, and offered in real time. You become awakened to the things that make you smile and they will make your heart be filled with thanksgiving and joy. And to that I say, gracias! Thank you.

CHALLENGE #9: Ignite Your Gratitude

Challenge number nine is for you to take account of all of your blessings in life. In your journal, jot down everything that you are thankful for. Write down the people in your life, the material goods you possess, and the experiences you have had that you appreciate. We all have things that are a blessing. When we have an attitude of gratitude it will make us happier. I encourage you to do this activity seasonally, four times throughout the year. During the tough times it will help us put things in perspective and during the moments we are soaring, gratitude will give even more lift to our wings. Be thankful.

"There is power in prayer. When men work, they work. But when men pray, God works."

-Angus Buchan

CHAPTER 21: Power of Prayer & Divine Connection

The trip was going well. My estimated time of arrival was about 9am. After picking up my friend Andrew in Syracuse, we would be on our way and in Buffalo for the football game with plenty of time to enjoy a fun tailgate amidst the Bills mafia outside of the confines of Ralph Wilson Stadium. Like many long car trips, I started it out by gathering up my thoughts and prayer intentions. On my mind and in my heart today was my family and a couple of friends, who had been going through tough times lately. I pulled my rosary out of my pocket, made the sign of the cross and then laid out the intentions I had thought of beforehand, those which struck my heart.

The weather on this particular Sunday in late December was fairly warm for upstate New York, 41 degrees with some rain. I drove my black Toyota Corolla, the first car I had ever owned outright, at a decent pace. I had set the cruise control for 65 mph to accomodate for the rain. I said the *Apostles Creed* and then began the *Our Father* and saying the *Hail Mary's*. While praying each decade of the rosary, I called to mind the intentions and also meditated on the mystery of Christ's life. Since it was a Sunday, I was praying the *glorious mysteries* of the rosary, which include the resurrection from the dead, ascension into Heaven, descent of the Holy Spirit on Pentecost, assumption of the Blessed Mother, and coronation of Mary, Queen of Heaven. As I was half way through the third decade or set of beads, I felt a weird vibration and my car began to shake. I looked down and noticed that suddenly, the temperature had drastically plummeted. It was now 33 degrees and ice was gathering instantly on my windshield.

I began to slow my pace, but then out of nowhere, my car began to have a mind of its own and unexpectedly began to fish tail and slide. I had hit a patch of black ice. I looked to my right and there was an 18 wheeler adjacent to my small sedan on the interstate. Fear started to set in as my car continued to slide, crossing the lined barrier on the road and headed directly for the big rig. I was a second away from going underneath and being crushed to death. I grabbed the wheel harder than ever before and yanked it forcefully to the left, while slamming my foot onto the break. Simultaneously, as the 18 wheeler glided by, what happened next over the following few seconds seemed to last a lifetime. My car spun around like a top, circling the entire lane of traffic I had been in, then again it shot around doing another 360. I hit a second patch of black ice and was launched into a frenzy of barrel rolls, flipping two and a half times, ultimately landing upside down in a roadside ditch.

The events happened so quickly and so violently, with such a great force and yet everything came to a halt in my mind resorting to slow motion. Inside my brain, like a movie scene playing out, I saw my wife, my parents, my brother, a flash of my grandparents and then there was this thought and prayer...God, If I don't survive this crash, please let all of those I care about know that I love them and allow them to be able to overcome this tragedy. Take me to you if I don't emerge alive.

When the car finally came to rest alongside a huge snow bank, I was hanging upside down with only my seatbelt holding me in place. I was conscious because I had what seemed to be most of my senses. I opened my eyes and could see, but I didn't know if I was severely injured or bleeding. I touched my face and my head and I did not feel any blood. Did I have any broken bones or any other injuries? I moved my arms and my legs and they felt okay. Now, I began to panic a bit and thought I must get out of this car as soon as I can just in case it is on fire or in the middle of the road. The windshield was shattered, the roof was smashed in, every door and window was completely obliterated. How was I going to escape? Finally I recognized that the rear passenger side door appeared to be operable. I unbuckled my seat belt and dropped down a few feet as my car was upside down... Thud! Then I climbed over the center console and into the back seat trying to avoid glass and debris. I reached for the back door handle and popped it open. I could hear cars racing by. Next, I crawled out the car and onto the ground. I was alive and away from danger.

While I gathered myself and attempted to stand on my feet, as if she dropped down straight from Heaven, a New York State Trooper was literally three feet from me. I got up in a daze and she said, "Wow, I watched your entire accident. It is amazing that you do not have a single scratch on your body, let alone that you are alive." She was absolutely right. I was so lucky. And then I realized, it wasn't luck at all. I opened my right hand and lifted the beads up to her and said, "This is why." I showed her my rosary. The Blessed Mother and good Lord surely were watching out for me on that gloomy and treacherous day. I know that I was protected with supernatural grace from above and that my life was spared. As I walked across the highway to get into the Trooper's car she told me again how lucky I was. She stressed that where my car went off the road was the perfect spot because if I hadn't hit the snow bank at that exact angle when I spun and flipped off the road, my car would have rolled over the center median and been a sitting duck for oncoming traffic. Talk about dodging a bullet. Wow, I was so blessed and lucky to be alive. It was then in that moment that I was again reminded that miracles do in fact happen every day.

Little did I know as the Trooper started to take down some of my information and double check to ensure that I was alright that at least four other accidents had taken place on that same strip of black ice. That stretch of about a quarter mile on the highway that morning was lethal. The Trooper said, we had to go to the next accident and see if the people were okay. The two other cars and a pickup truck were off the road, having slid from the highway into the snow bank, but nothing serious. The final accident was the white 18 wheeler, the same one that had passed me as I spun out of control. The driver had gone into the guardrail and his gargantuan vehicle was inoperable. My heart was still racing and I was shell shocked. Never in my life had I experienced something so terrifying and completely out of my control. To think that a half second later, a couple more inches, or any other variable and I could have been on a coroner's table being prepared to go six feet under. That is a scary thought for anyone, let alone when you are only in your mid 20s with the rest of your life ahead of you.

Prayer is the act of talking to God or communicating with the divine. Wooden beads and a cross never had so much power and meaning in my life as it did in the days that followed. See, growing up, my great grandmother, Nanny DelPozzo, was the only person I knew who prayed the rosary. As a young boy, my dad would take me to mass early on Sunday mornings. We would go to pick up my great grandparents at their house on the Hill, our family compound, and then drive a few miles to Resurrection Parish in Germantown. During the car ride, Nanny Delpozzo would always be holding her rosary beads, pressing her wrinkled fingers on each one. As she whispered the prayers to herself, she would look over at me and smile. She was always at peace, as well as my great grandpa. They had something special inside. I guess that is what over 60 years of marriage and a big faith filled Italian family will do. After mass per tradition, we would always go back to my great grandparents' small house and they would bring out something sweet to eat. We talked about the week ahead and shared, making some amazing memories.

As I drove back away from the accident and watched my car being pulled out the ditch, flipped back over, and lifted on top of a huge flatbed, I shook my head and smiled. Close call. The power of prayer cannot be underestimated. This example from my own life is just one instance, one drop in the bucket, when God has shown up, and He showed up in an extraordinary way. Jesus assured the apostles and his disciples that if they had even the smallest measure of faith they would see God working tremendously in their lives. In the Gospel the Lord expressed with great fervor, "Ask and it will be given to you, seek and you will find, knock and the door will be opened to you. For everyone who asks, receives, the one who seeks, finds, and the one who knocks the door is opened." (Matthew 7:7). I realized while praying the *Hail Mary* I had been protected. The very words "Pray for us sinners, now and at the hour of our death, Amen," had literally come into play for me on that December morning. Thankfully, by the grace of God, I had escaped the hour of my death, which had been knocking. I was kept safe and death wasn't allowed to enter in. Over the next few months, I began to pray the rosary every day. I offered up my intentions each morning and the measure of faith I had continued to increase. Years later, I have not missed a single day of praying the rosary. My call on the intercession of the Blessed Mother each morning sets the tone for the day and truly is my protection.

    I was deep in prayer at the Cathedral of our Lady of Guadalupe in Mexico City when I felt God leading me to become a missionary and start a program in our Diocese. Each day I like to take time to quiet myself, allow God to speak to me, and share with Him what is on my heart. This is good for the soul.

Over the last few years I have witnessed the Lord working in profound and miraculous ways. One summer I was scuba diving in a lake in the Adirondacks. I was deep down beneath the surface when I felt tension and a weird sensation on my air line. I began to swim up to the surface because oxygen was no longer flowing from my tank to my mask. Before I could resurface; however, I recognized that I was trapped between a dock and some large rocks. I could not see as the water was opaque. The lake was extremely dark in this area below the surface with a large amount of seaweed and other debris. I turned to prayer and began the *Hail Mary*. My heart was pounding out of my chest and as I prayed, in my mind, I grew more calm. Increased breath infiltrated my lungs and I was given more time. Suddenly, I felt a tug. Something or some force pulled me to the left and I swam that way. Out of the blue I was set free and trapped no longer. I surfaced and tore my mask off with a fury gasping for air. Wow, was that a close call. Another answered prayer.

Now there are situations in life, there is news we hear, there are circumstances that almost stifle us to the point that we forget to or cannot pray. It is during these moments that we must call on God the most for help. I remember a time that my friend was given such devastating news. Michelle discovered after the 20 week ultrasound that her little girl was severely deformed. She had a genetic chromosomal disorder and the doctors said they should abort the baby. My friend was so distraught with raw emotion, tears cascading from her face. She was told that the best case scenario, if the baby survived a live birth, would be severe mental retardation and being born without any limbs. My initial response was to console Michelle and her family. I began to pray that they would still have the child. Every day I attended morning mass and dedicated a rosary for that baby's healing and well being. A few months later, after weeks upon weeks of offering up daily mass for this child, little Hannah was born into the world.

Much to the surprise of the team of doctor's who had already diagnosed all of the handicaps and developmental disabilities that would surely impinge this newborn child for as long as she lived, she came into this world prematurely yet as healthy as can be. Now a few years later, Hannah sits on her parents' laps, plays with her sisters, and is seen by everyone smiling the brightest smile. This little girl is the absolute joy of her parents' lives. She attends pre-school and is the happiest and healthiest little ball of energy who has nothing wrong with her at all. I came to find out that her name, Hannah, the very name her parents chose for her, means "favour" or "she who is filled with God's grace." Prayer, it is the remedy and medicine that can heal. For doctors do not have the final say and diagnosis, only God does. Nothing is impossible for God... "And he said, 'What is impossible for human beings is possible for God.'" (Luke 18:27) My hope is that through the power of prayer your hope will remain and carry you on.

I share these powerful stories because prayer works. Jesus listens and our loving Father in Heaven wants to see His children trust in Him. We have an Advocate in the Holy Spirit that was sent to us after Christ ascended to teach us and guide us in all things. The Mother of our Lord, our Mother, Mary, protects the Church and desires us to draw near to her so she can lead us closer to the Sacred Heart of Jesus. The forces and powers of the Heavens, God's angels and the saints are praying for us and lifting us up. I encourage you to pay heed to these powerful words of Christ himself, "If you remain in me and my words remain in you, ask whatever you wish, and it will be done for you." (John 15:7) By remaining faithful, by following and living a life of love for God and others, we just need to ask and it will be done for us. Can you actually comprehend and wrap your mind around this bold and deep statement? These words carry such great clout. If we simply stay close to the Lord and ask, consider it done. Wow! As mind blowing and as rooted as this promise is, it is so true. But if we waver and have even the slightest doubt or if we go astray and do not stay close to the Lord, then certainly the prayer we make will not be answered.

My hope is that through spiritual growth and maturity, as your relationship with the Lord blossoms, the essence of your prayer will go from asking small to asking big! Even more so, I hope that your prayer becomes more of a conversation with God than request upon request. "Pray without ceasing," as St. Paul urged the members of the early church. In doing so we grow closer to God and the love, grace, mercy, and beauty of our creator becomes ever more instilled in us. The qualities and characteristics of Christ Jesus permeate our hearts, minds, and souls as we set out to be the hands and feet of the Lord to bring hope to a broken and down trodden world. Then and only then will we be at true and full peace. As the great Saint Augustine so vigorously proclaimed, "Our hearts are restless until they rest in you, Oh God."

There are certain circumstances and situations that we face that require an absolute miracle. Miracles happen every day. I cannot tell you how many times I have heard people discussing the topic of miracles and that they didn't understand why in Jesus' time, there were so many miracles happening. Certainly the Lord had a ton to do with them and part of His way to gain followers and transform the world was through miraculous works. Unfortunately, in the 21st Century most people believe miracles are dead. I believe that miracles are happening right before our very eyes and that there are so many unexplainable happenings that radically change our lives and the lives of others. It is just a matter of noticing them and understanding the power of God in everyday experiences. By definition, a miracle is *a surprising and welcome event that is not explicable by natural or scientific laws and is therefore considered to be the work of a divine agency.* The one thing that has always really blown me away was that shortly before Jesus left the earth he referenced his miraculous power working in and through common people. The Lord said, "Amen, amen, I say to you, whoever believes in me will do the works that I do, and will do greater ones than these, because I am going to the Father." (John 14:12) Think about that and allow it to sink in. We will do *greater* works than those that Jesus himself did on this earth! Now that is something to get excited about. That is something to fire you up and realize that miracles are happening in our world today and will continue to happen. What is required is for us to believe. Whether it be the saving of lives, the personal transformation of an individual, a small or a large God moment, a healing, or any other example of amazing grace, miracles are real and they are alive! As I have mentioned with examples from my own life, miracles do happen. Do you believe in miracles? I hope so because sometimes we face times in life when this is exactly what we need.

    The power of prayer is mighty and later on in the next section we will discuss the importance of divine connections. Before moving on, I wanted to take a few minutes to share with you some other miraculous moments and times when God revealed himself to me in beautiful ways. The purpose of sharing these with you is to brag on the Lord and to share his goodness. It is to help us recognize that the Lord is present and continuing to work in our lives. In a world that is consumed with trouble, a society that is bombarded with bad news on almost every television broadcast, and in a day and age where so often people wonder where God is, it is important to reflect on the good. For me, nothing has been more powerful or necessary than going to the Lord and praying before him in the Blessed Sacrament. When my heart is hurting, I am at my wits end, or I need an answer, I have learned to run to Jesus. As a Catholic I believe that Jesus is fully present in the Eucharist. When we receive him in Holy Communion, he enters us and is alive within us. Christ gave us this great sacrament at the last supper when he proclaimed, "I am the bread of life; whoever comes to me will never hunger, and whoever believes in me will never thirst... I am the living bread that came down from heaven; whoever eats this bread will live forever; and the bread that I will give is my flesh for the life of the world.... Whoever eats my flesh and drinks my blood has eternal life, and I will raise him on the last day. (John 6:35, 51, 54) Jesus wants us to come to him and as we discussed previously, he thirsts for us. At many moments in my life I have been overwhelmed by the weight of the world. However, by receiving the Lord in the Eucharist at mass or by going to sit in the quiet of the chapel, Christ has consoled me. In these quiet moments when my trust was tested most and I was in need of a miracle, God would settle my uneasy heart and whisper loving things to me. However, there have been a few times when Jesus showed up in extremely powerful ways. These are the moments I want to share and discuss because God is fully alive and present today, just as he was thousands of years ago.

In August of 2012 I was at a Catholic youth camp in Wurtsboro, NY, Camp Veritas. It was near the end of a long week when we had spent countless hours with middle school and highschool aged kids playing all kinds of sports, participating in mass together, and having heard so many great faith based talks. I had some troubles in my heart at the time. I felt some pain from things I was struggling with and there were numerous people in my family who were hurting. During adoration, when the Blessed Sacrament was exposed and I spent quiet time with the Lord in prayer something unexplainable and remarkable happened. I was deep in prayer, pouring out my troubles to the Lord and speaking to him all the things that were weighing me down. I had always been told as a kid that someday we will see God face to face in Heaven, but no one sees him until then. It was what it was, like it or not. But during that occasion of prayer, I opened my eyes and looked really hard at Christ in the Eucharistic host. Hundreds of times in my life, perhaps even thousands, I have sat in prayer before the Lord in the Blessed Sacrament and looked at him, hidden and veiled on the altar behind the form of a tiny wafer. I had my doubts in the past if this was really Jesus, but had come to believe that he truly was there, masked behind the essence of bread. It was during this time of deep and intense prayer that for but a second, I saw the face of the Lord. I could see the image and face of Jesus looking back at me. He had his crown of thorns on and was looking back sorrowful. But then his look turned to a smile and intense peace and joy filled my heart. His loving gaze assured me that I was loved. This was an experience I did not know how to comprehend. I wrote it down in a journal, but shared it with no one because I did not think anyone would believe me. I prayed and asked God what this meant and he spoke to my heart. One day I would tell others when the time was right, that day happens to be today and why I am sharing it with you.

What I did not realize was that this intense encounter with

the Lord would not be the last time I would have such a powerful experience with Jesus. Over the years, Christ has revealed himself in some mysterious ways to me and to many others. What I have come to believe and understand is that this happens when we trust him with all of our heart, we believe fully in his power, and that he appears to us when we need it most. In the summer of 2016, my wife was about to enter a new phase of a career where she would be away for the next six months due to training coming that fall. I had begun that summer volunteering at the local city mission where I would spend at least three nights a week serving the poor. At the same time I had a number of family members going through some really hard things that were again weighing on my heart. So, I went before the Lord in mid July during an evening and spent time with God once again. The Lord appeared to me for the second time in the Blessed Sacrament. I felt God's intense presence and he assured me that everything would be okay. Over the next six months my faith would be radically tested, but it would never waver. God helped me through being separated from my wife due to different locations and our marriage would become stronger than ever. Only God can do this. I believe that the moment I saw the Lord the second time in the Blessed Sacrament was because I said, "Jesus I trust in you." It was then, when I fully trusted and laid it all out at the foot of his cross, that Christ revealed himself to me and touched my heart.

We will now fast forward to 2019. This particular year was another trying and large year of transition in my life. My uncle had gotten really sick, I was discerning what career change to make, and was really wrestling with God in my heart. I was not at peace teaching or with the climate of my school and knew that there was so much uncertainty ahead in my future. While coaching at catholic basketball camp toward the end of July that summer, I decided to share my faith testimony with about 100 campers and 15 or so coaches. I poured out my heart to those in that hot gymnasium and shared all the good that God had done in my life. I explained how God had transformed my life, spared me from myself, and that he opened doors that I never could have imagined. I intentionally spent time on sharing the power of prayer, particularly the importance of having a devotion to saying the rosary daily by asking for the intercession of Mary. It was that afternoon that I shared with them about Our Lady of Guadalupe and the miracles God worked through her with her appearance to St. Juan Diego in 1531. If you do not know the events that took place, I highly encouraged you to read about it. It is yet another powerful testament to God's power, love, and saving grace. Two days later, after leading the entire camp in the rosary, Jesus appeared smiling to me in the face of the Eucharist during adoration. It was at this moment when I literally saw the face of Christ smiling, that I received peace in my heart. Christ's face then turned to sorrow and he was crying. At that moment I felt the Lord urge me to pray for those who were broken, for the sick, and for our hurting world. I prayed and kept staring at the Lord. His face changed from sorrow to joy and he was then smiling back at me. A tremendous warmth came over me and enveloped my body and soul. I felt as if I was floating for a few seconds as intense peace flooded my heart yet again. All I could do was thank God and praise him.

Later that same year in the fall of 2019, I was a couple of months into my prison ministry. Each week I would travel about 40 minutes south to a prison in Greene County. As a ministry leader, I had the privilege of working with incarcerated men who desired to get back on track. What I learned was that hearts can change and God can transform "monsters" into saints. Out of the 900 or so prisoners, only a few would come every week to our faith sharing and bible study sessions. For an hour each Thursday, we opened the scriptures, shared where Jesus was present in our lives, discussed challenges and heartache, and spoke of forgiveness. Over the next year, I witnessed a number of these men have a radical change of heart. They admitted that they deserved every minute of the time they faced behind bars and were deeply sorry for the wrong they did. Their hearts hurt because they recognized they had hurt others. They knew they were broken and understood the Lord could make them whole. One man named Drey really stuck out to me. He said, "Sometimes in life we need God to wake us up. Sometimes he will do it with a hammer. Other times he will use a sledgehammer. But for me, he used a jack hammer." Drey opened up to me and his trust in God was remarkable. He said, "I know that I needed to come to prison so my life would be saved." During a number of occasions as we held hands after the faith sharing session was completed and we closed out in prayer, I felt God's intense presence. It was as if Jesus was truly in the room and standing with us in the circle as we said the Lord's prayer. The Holy Spirit was present in that place. What I have learned is that there is no place on this earth that God will not go and at times he will speak to us through the most unlikely people and the most mysterious circumstances. The Lord's messengers came in all shapes, sizes, and forms. We must remain open and look through eyes of faith.

Lastly, it was nearing Christmas time and I was troubled by some more disturbing news. On December 13, 2019, my uncle, who I dearly loved, was taken to Albany Medical Center and had to have an emergency surgery to remove lesions on his brain after a rare fungus had attacked him. That morning he went in and got his MRI and scan. The doctors found the complications a little after 10:15 am that morning. At the same time of my uncle's appointment and diagnosis, I was still teaching and was in school during the middle of my English lesson. All of a sudden, I started feeling light headed and dizzy. My heart became heavy and I felt that something was gravely wrong. Later on in the day I went to the adoration chapel after learning that my uncle would need surgery. It was after speaking to my mom who had relayed the news to me once school ended that I understood why during the middle of my lesson I felt the very life sucked out of me. At that moment in time my uncle received his diagnosis. Some call it a coincidence, I call it a Godcidence. After I was able to leave work, I drove straight to the church to spend time in prayer. When my uncle was in surgery at 4:30pm, I prayed a rosary for him and asked Jesus for healing. We needed a miracle. When I was praying and gazing at the Lord in the most Blessed Sacrament, I saw the face of Jesus in the Eucharist and Christ was crying. A tear was streaming down the side of the Lord's face and left cheek. Jesus was wearing a ring on his finger and then put his finger over his mouth and told me to quiet my heart and know that he (my uncle) would not die. He told me that eventually he would be okay. Jesus spoke this to my heart and then went back behind the host in the form of the little wafer in the monstrance. I was taken back by yet another powerful and mysterious encounter. The only person I told was my wife. I did not know if she would believe me, as it was so hard to explain. I felt our Lord's overwhelming presence and the warmth of the Holy Spirit engulf my soul and my whole body for a few seconds was filled with intense peace when I saw Jesus crying for my family.

So what does all of this mean? Why did God reveal himself to me in some profound ways? Will I experience God's intense love and presence in my life again and see him face to face? That I do not know. What I do know and believe is that Christ's love for us is intense. He realizes our heartache and our pain. He knows when we need supernatural grace and experiences of his overwhelming love to console us. The Lord understands the burdens we carry and wants us to run to him. Jesus is always there for us, waiting with open arms. He is ready to receive us and to help us with our every need. In times of uncertainty, we have to do two things, we must wait and we must pray. As the disciples did centuries ago, we must enter the upper room and fall on our knees in front of the Lord. When we pray, if we believe fully, then God will hear us. Our prayer will be answered and Christ will show up in our lives. At times the Lord will come in ways that are ordinary and explainable and at other times mysterious and peculiar occurrences. The best part is that it doesn't take immense faith to feel God's presence or to know that he is there with us, but simply faith the size of a tiny mustard seed. Christ will console us and we will be able to get through whatever we are facing. We must pray and believe.

Divine Connections

Furthermore, prayer is deeply rooted and helps us to establish divine connections. During the duration of my life I have been the recipient of tremendous and amazingly divine connections. God's way of interweaving the very fabric of my life with the most unlikely and interesting people has blown me away. The examples of divine connectivity around us are so great and innumerable that even the stars of the sky cannot compare in summation. When you think back and reflect on life and how things came to be, where and how you met your friends, and who has powerfully touched your life in a memorable way, it is dynamic in nature.

The chain of events and web of connections run deep for me personally. One "yes" leads to a series of events and happenings that then point to an escapade of other developments. All the while, where we meet so many new people along the way, this adds up to create the crux of our life and our relationships. Some of those folks will indeed be one hit wonders, or merely a stranger passing in the night. While others turn into our friends, and still some become true gems that add such depth to our lives. These people become our true amigos.

On a service learning trip in Dominica, a Caribbean Island south of Antigua, I spent ten days on a mission with the poor. We served by teaching in a school for the handicapped, as well as working and playing with children at a youth center. Our group stayed in humble quarters and during my free time each day I would take a mile or so walk to the local homeless shelter and spend time with the elderly there. In the evenings we had our service learning class where we did some readings and reflections and examined the day. When I signed up to be part of the Lead Learning Community at Le Moyne College during my freshman orientation, I did not realize I would have such a powerful experience with my classmates. Nor did I ever imagine in a thousand years that three of the twenty or so college students on the trip would become not only my best friends, but a groomsman in my wedding party, my best man, and my lovely wife! Not to mention, as a little icing on the cake, the professor and trip leader happened to be a Jesuit priest who celebrated my wedding mass. Pretty cool.

So how did this all come to be? Well, it is funny. Because I said, "Yes" to go on the trip two years later than normal, all of these doors opened up and divine connections were made. More simply put, it was God's plan. Freshmen at Le Moyne were the exclusive group invited to go on the Dominica service trip. I was a junior at the time, out of place, but it was meant to be. Back during my freshman year I applied for the mission experience to Kenya. This was the most popular and sought after mission trip our college offered for upperclassmen. Only ten people from a campus community just shy of 3,000 would be able to attend. Never had a freshman gone before. Also, I was "supposed to" go on the Dominica trip as part of the first year student Lead Learning Community requirements. An exception was made and my application was accepted. Jambo or hello as they say in Swahili! I had been invited to board the plane and go to Kenya. When I look back at my life, this was just the beginning and the tip of the iceberg when it came to divine connections. If I had gone to Dominica my freshman year, which was the norm and expectation, I never would have gone two years later. I likely wouldn't have met the group members two classes below me including my wife and wedding party filled with life long friends.

There is so much more to this personal story of mine by uttering a simple, "yes." I agreed to go on a hike in Dominica on a whim to a boiling lake with one other member of the group, Andrew, who is now my best friend. Also, my girlfriend at the time broke up with me directly after the trip out of left field, which opened up an avenue to pursue a girl who caught my eye in Dominica. This was a girl right from Albany, less than an hour drive from my house, who I hadn't known. This young lady I had only seen one time prior. Oh yeah, that girl is now my wife! The divine connections keep growing as my wife's mom had a friend who helped me secure my first teaching job at KIPP Tech Valley Charter School where I worked for eight years.

Additionally, this connection and new job also led me to move to the capital region, where I got plugged into my current parish,

St. Pius X and am blessed to serve in so many capacities. It was during the bible study I ran on Tuesday nights that a member who hadn't come in a while brought a friend of his, on one random evening. I could tell there was something different about this guy, he had a super strong and deep faith. We hit it off after the study and talked for a while. Fast forward to present day, we are good friends and I work for Garrett's business with his brother Nick at NOVUS Clothing Company. Oh and if it cannot get better, wait, it does. That connection with the new bible study member, who just so happens to be a former Focus Missionary, led me on my next mission trip to Mexico City. That divine connection led to my passion and mission work that I do with Hope of the Poor as a missionary, as well as my involvement with Baseball Miracles, which continue to allow me to serve children and the poor throughout the world today.

Serving in Mexico City with Hope of the Poor & Baseball Miracles as a missionary has been an incredible experience.

Visiting and serving the poor in the city dump has allowed me to meet amazing people like Michael and encounter Jesus face to face.

I now fully grasp the depth of love, it is found in the little ones.

Divine connections are happening all the time. God is lining up the right people and the right opportunities for you and me well in advance. He continues to pave the way. Remain faithful and say, "yes." Surround yourself with quality people and take part in some noble activities and you will see some amazing things transpire in your life. It is only a matter of time! Soon you too will come face to face with the divine. It is so interesting that the Lord shows up in so many forms and in so many ways, most often being manifested in the appearance of average everyday people like you and like me. Who knows how you will change someone else's life, that is up to God to decide. What I do know is that divine connections will astound you and they will lead you to where you need to be.

"It is not the size of a man but the size of his heart that matters."

-Evander Holyfield

CHAPTER 22: Final Shot

"You miss 100 percent of the shots you don't take." – Wayne Gretzky

The clock was winding down, not much time left in the game. We had drawn the play up and it was now a matter of execution. The score was tied and the ball was swung to the opposite side. The seconds began to wane. 10, 9, 8, 7, 6, 5, 4,...the pass came his way. He ran off a screen and took the shot...3, 2 the ball went through the net, a complete swish! Seconds later, the game was over and the bench erupted. Thousands in the crowd at the Dome dressed in Orange were stunned as Syracuse had been defeated by Le Moyne. David had slayed Goliath and a massive celebration took place for the Dolphins.

Being part of that winning team was phenomenal and something I will always remember. What it brings to mind; however, is that the final shot must not be taken prematurely. We must trust the process, listen to our coach, and carry out the play. On April 14, 2006 my story could have ended. It saddens me to think I almost took a premature shot and call it quits on life. But here I am today, standing tall and before you. I am here not because of my own doing, but because the Lord desired it and I am honored and humbled to tell you what He has done in my life. I pray that you too will brag on the Lord to those around you as you share the miraculous power of Him in your own life.

Why we face the Cross and the Friday moments in our life is hard to understand now. Many of us will probably ask God for some answers when we meet Him someday. Remember, God can turn any hardship or difficulty around. The Lord can shift the powers in your life and turn anything into something amazing. I encourage you, when the opportunity comes and God speaks to your heart, that you are able to share your story. It may be with a close friend or loved one at first. It might be in a park when you meet a stranger and God puts it on your heart. Or it could be through a book or another platform, where you have an audience. No matter what and no matter the way you are led to share, your story is important and can change lives.

There is great power in sharing what God has done in our lives because sometimes it is what others need. Your witness is immense in this time and space and you are the "light of the world" and "the salt of the earth." So let your light shine before others and always know you do not walk this road alone. Your answer is one prayer away. Be moved by God's love in your life so we can be more loving toward ourselves and others. Then we will be more concerned and take Extreme Ownership of our lives. We will put away excuses and throw aside the blame. We will be able to conquer the darkness and trouble we face in order to walk in victory toward the light. The fire within us will burn brightly again. In the book "Extreme Ownership," written by Jacko Willinik and Leaf Babin (Navy Seals) they state, *"Total responsibility for failure is a difficult thing to accept and taking ownership when things go wrong takes extraordinary humility and courage. But by doing just that it is an absolute necessity to learn and to grow and improve."* Let me remind you one final time that God says, "I have set before you, life and death, blessing and the curse. Choose life, that you and your descendents might live." (Deuteronomy 30:19). Whether it is in your control or not, God desires you to come to Him so you can have the life He has planned for you. Whether your state and lot in life at this moment is positive and going great, or is in the valley of despair; you are deeply loved and desired.

When we trust and believe, this allows us to be more open-minded. We can then more trustingly ask God for his help and do the best with the cards we are dealt when difficulty comes our way and we face Friday Moments. The choice is ours. When the weight of the world comes upon us, we can choose to shut God out or let him in. We can turn away from the one who created us and desires us to be filled with joy and peace or we can walk toward him despite our challenges. It is up to us to allow Him in so that His power and grace can flood our souls and heart. It is my experience and belief that His love and divine assistance can and will carry us through the darkness and into the light.

Remember that nothing great comes easy and that when we grow in our faith we will do so by enduring struggle. We may fall often, but we can always rise again with God's help. Fall and get up again. Do not stay down instead think, "Nunc Coepi." I encourage you to be determined and be relentless. What do you want? Dream, imagine, and set goals for your future. Pray for it and believe. Trust and the Lord can make it happen. Go after it and attack it. Do not be the gazelle running away, scared and afraid. Be the Lion on the prowl, devour your troubles, and take down your hardship. Be a beast and slay the enemy when He comes your way in whatever form he shows up as. Be an overcomer and it will happen.

Life can hurt and we might hurt others, but God forgives. God knows we are not perfect but asks us to try again. When we forgive ourselves and believe in the new life He offers, then others will see a change and forgive us in time. God will empower us, He will build us back up. Jesus is the bridge between us and the Father. He stands in our place and makes us worthy. When Friday comes, know that in due time the Resurrection is on it's way. When darkness creeps in and is surrounding you, know that the light is closer than ever and is ready to crack through. You are loved and His Grace will supply your every need. Stay the course, finish the race and "do not grow tired of doing good, for in due time you shall reap the harvest if you do not give up." (Gal 6:9) God bless you and may the resurrection of our Lord Jesus Christ empower you to conquer the cross & walk humbly with your God.

"A champion is defined not by their wins but by how they can recover when they fall."

-Serena Williams

CHAPTER 23: Living the Dream

Over a decade ago it was a mere pipe dream that I would be 31 years old, married, have a successful job in business, and be well known in my community. I say this not out of braggadocious nature, but out of immense gratitude and awe. The course of life has continued to amaze me as time marches by. The Lord has not only shown up time and time again, but He has showed out. God has made it well known to me what is possible with faith and determination. When we spend time reviewing the path of our lives this becomes very clear and evident. Who we were or what we struggled with years ago is sometimes hard to believe now that we are in a much different state in life. This re emphasizes the power of new beginnings and how personal growth takes place over time. It also is a reminder that the fire that burns within, namely Christ's light, can illuminate a new path we would have never imagined. Our very dreams will often fall short, not because they didn't come to pass, but instead there was something even greater than we could imagine for our future.

Dreams are important. We need to have them and it is healthy to think big. Some people might think that it is pointless to dream, well they are missing out. In order for amazing happenings to occur, we first must dream. Then we work hard, remain faithful, and so often we will be living the dream as a reality. After all, it is dreams that have become a reality that have transformed our world. Dreams lived out and accomplished show us what is possible when one sets goals and dedicates their life and energy for the cause they believe in. The essential component is dreaming and taking action. Dreams without action are a mere wish. Unless you live in a fantasy world or in a Disney movie, wishes aren't coming true on their own. Dreams that are worked toward, kept present on one's mind and in one's heart, and prayed with, pack great power. These cherished aspirations are what we desire. So dream big and move the needle to make it come true.

Today, I am a man on a mission. God has opened up new doors to me that I could have never expected. Unimaginable blessings have chased me down. They are going to chase you down too. A few years ago I read a book by legendary NCAA basketball announcer, Dick Vitale. The title of Dicky V's book was *Living the Dream*. He wrote all about how his life got turned upside down after he coached Detroit University and took a head coaching job with the Detroit Pistons in the NBA. He went from on top of the world of sports to the bottom of the dunghill. Vitale, who is known for his prominent voice, his enthusiasm and his super high energy, turned inward and dug deep. He utilized this door that closed and this hardship in his life to seek out a new path and a new opportunity. He had a dream to inspire, to reach others, and make a difference in the world of sports. Over the next couple of years, Dick Vitale grabbed life by the horns, set the ball in motion, and made that dream happen.

After his coaching days came to a close, Dicky V took a leap of faith into the world of broadcasting with a new company known as ESPN. You might have heard of them before. At the time, they were certainly not the "world wide leader in sports." Vitale began by announcing on the radio an array of obscure sports and did not know what the future held. He stuck it out and stayed the course, keeping the faith and carrying on. Over the next few years Vitale made a name for himself through hard work and his way with people. His love of life was contagious and it led him to soon be on television calling some of the biggest games. The years went on and ESPN grew and grew, ballooning to become the number one sports channel and network in the world.

Vitale speaks about getting the "ziggy" or being fired from the Pistons and how detrimental it was to his career as a coach that came to a crashing halt. He endured the pain and an unknown future. Now he is, in his own words, truly "living the dream." Dicky V is seen on the air all the time. Before the game he broadcasts on ESPN Vitale is crowd surfing, wearing crazy costumes in the student section, taking pictures with fans, and watching the best games each week from a courtside seat. No wonder why he says things like, "It's Awesome baby with a capital A!"

My favorite sports announcer, Dick Vitale and I before the Syracuse game against Duke at the Carrier Dome in 2017.

To live the dream, we often have to endure the nightmare first or some kind of let down. We must not get discouraged, and have to be able to bounce back and rebound in life. So many great opportunities and possibilities are out there. We must always trust the process, keep our foot on the gas pedal, and continue to have our head held high. The only dream that is dead is one that we fall asleep on or give up on.

When you wake up from a great dream it breathes some life into you. It makes you smile before you even jump out of bed to start the day. But that dream you had last night will be soon forgotten and it will become a thing of the past. Dreams are much better and more enjoyable when they come true. You cannot merely dream, you must decide to do whatever is in your power to make your dreams become a reality. Listen to these words of wisdom by Michael Jordan, "Some people want it to happen, some wish it would happen, and others make it happen."

Hopefully you will continue to dream big and you will keep your focus in order to live the best life that is out there for your taking. Then you will not just be living, but you will truly be alive. Today it's time to thrive. Remember that no matter where you were or what you went through, that doesn't define who you are or what your life will become. Camilla Eyring Kimball put it in perspective best by saying, "You do not find the happy life. You make it." You have the final say. Go get it and make your dream life come true! Find the way, get on top of the wave, and ride it. Make your dreams your reality! Personally, I have conquered many mountains in my life, each one has made me stronger and ignited my fire burning inside. My dreams are what often carry me on.

CHALLENGE #10: Make your Dreams your Reality

Congratulations! You made it to the final challenge and are almost at the end of the book. I have saved the very best for last. Your tenth challenge is to make your dreams your reality. Take out that list you created back in challenge #5. Reassess those aspirations and create a plan for you to begin making those dreams come true. Think about what you need to begin doing today, what changes must you make, and who can you call on to help you or hold you accountable? This is your life. Your future self will thank you for putting in the hard work it will take to reshape and take complete control over your future. It won't be easy, but you have what it takes to make your dream your reality!

"Blessed is the man who perseveres during temptation, for when he has withstood the test, he will receive the crown of life that God has promised to those who love him."

-James 1:12

CHAPTER 24: Claim Your Crown

It was time for the coronation. The moment we had all been waiting for. The prom was drawing to a close and my buddy was ready to find out who would be chosen as king and queen. Having the opportunity to volunteer at Tim Tebow's worldwide and annual event called *Night To Shine* was amazing. Witnessing hundreds of young adults with special needs get all dressed up in tuxedos and gowns, seeing them walk the red carpet, and take limo rides around town was tremendous. The pure joy in sharing a four course meal with my buddy, Tommy, who I sponsored for the night was awesome. We danced the night away and had an absolute blast! Tommy like the rest of the young people were plagued with diseases and disabilities, but that didn't stop them. This was their moment, this was truly their time to shine. I remember him anxiously awaiting the big announcement. Tommy said, "Hey Dan, who do you think will be crowned King?" I had already known what was about to happen, but I said to him, "Well, if it were up to me, you would certainly have my vote." Tommy gave me the biggest smile, followed by a high five. The master of ceremonies took the stage and approached the podium. All eyes and ears were locked on him as he opened the envelope to reveal the king and queen. He said at last, "We have decided tonight that you all are being crowned because you are all royalty in God's eyes." What a message and what a time for these young people. It was truly a moment they would never forget. I took a crown off the table they wheeled out and placed it on Tommy. I crowned him king of the night.

My Buddy, Tommy and I at Tim Tebow's *Night to Shine* in February 2020 after he was crowned King!

See, for me it is a big deal to be able to tell my story. Being able to express my inner thoughts to others and now to you has always been important to me. What is even more important; however, is being able to live out my passions, encourage others, and share some words of inspiration. It has always been a lifelong goal of mine to write a book. The more I thought about it though, it was becoming more and more a far off fantasy. We say we are going to do a lot of things and most of the time we have good intentions. Yet, action is the only thing that turns dreams or desires into a reality. So, I decided to take the first step, which led us to where we are today. I encourage you to turn your distant dreams or obscure bucket list items, into whatever you desire them to be. The bottom line is sometimes we have to simply get to work and "just do it."

Setting goals for our lives is significant. Being our authentic selves is even more crucial so we can live the life for which we were created. I am grateful to have had the opportunity to share with you some important happenings in my own life. I certainly would not be the man and person that I am today if I hadn't gone through the difficulty and if I hadn't decided to rise above the challenges. It was important for me to take some risks and embrace opportunity when it knocked on my door. Although it has been quite a wild ride, I still believe that the best is yet to come. I know that I have much more to live for and improvements I need to make. Every day is a new challenge to grow and blossom. The beast inside of me is continuously being released and my fire that burns within me is being continuously ignited. I am stronger and more powerful than I once was, but I am not satisfied. I am hungry and thirsting for more. My outlook on life is much different today than it was a decade ago and that is a good thing. I am progressing and life continues to refine me.

My final word to you is to wake up every day and attack life. Be the very best that you can possibly be. In doing so you will leave your mark on the world. Most importantly do it for yourself because then you will be truly alive and you can thrive. Take chances, trust the process, pray often, and know that God is on your side. Do whatever you feel is right and what you are being called to. Aspire for greatness and to always be the best version of yourself no matter what the cost. Do not take "No" for an answer. Prove the critics wrong, but most importantly, believe in yourself and believe in the people who believe in you. You are amazing. You have such a uniqueness about you. Stop waiting for tomorrow or approval to go after your dreams. Do not limit yourself, and dream big. God has a way of directing our steps and path where even our dreams fall short of His goodness and all He will do in our lives. You only get one life to live, so live it to the fullest. Stop looking over your shoulder and being concerned with who is watching. If it is in your heart, it is in there for a reason. Live with boldness and conviction.

    The stage is yours, it is your time to shine. Use the doubters and naysayers as fuel to your already burning fire. Tap into that internal motivation and allow that to propel you. Give your all and work hard. No one can stop you. Believe and do what you are called to do. As St. Padre Pio said, "Love and do what you will." When you follow your heart and listen to the Spirit, you cannot go wrong. Difficulty will come, but do not back down. Be brave and courageous and take it on. You are more than an overcomer and have what it takes to defeat anything that you face. You are not in this alone. Remember, that God is on your side and is only a prayer away. Tune into your mind and use it as your greatest asset and strength. The finish line of life is still out there, keep running your race because victory is in store. Begin again if you fall and keep pushing forward. No matter what, know and believe that it is worth it.

    Go out there today and claim your crown! Victory is right around the corner. You have royal blood flowing through your veins, you are more than a conqueror, and this life is yours for the taking. God has created you and instilled in you everything that you need. You are more than adequate, you are fully loaded. You are a stick of dynamite ready to explode and leave your imprint on the world. You are fierce and hungry. You are a beast, a lion. Your past or how life started, the hurdles you have jumped over, the challenges you have endured; these have all strengthened you. You are running your own race, you are chasing down your goals, your desires, and your dreams. They are no longer far away. They are no longer distant fantasies. No, you are making them realities day by day. Your positivity, energy, enthusiasm for life is the fire that burns within you. Your faith has been ignited to a whole new level and the Spirit that drives you on the inside is propelling you into a new direction. Your destiny is being shaped and you are a co-pilot with God who has an amazing future ahead of you.

Like an athlete who desires to win the ultimate prize, you know that this will not be easy. There are sharks out there trying to stop you, just keep swimming and do not let your guard down. The negativity and noise will inevitably be cranked up and people will tell you what you don't want to hear. Life will toss curveball after curveball and you will be tempted to stop in your tracks. But you will not cease, you will not give in, and you will not stop moving forward. For the finish line is out there, your life is yours to live, and the crown that awaits you is worth it! The mountains seem tall at the bottom looking up and the valleys so treacherous to climb out of, yet you will carry on. You advance, you endure, you progress. You are a winner, there is no loser in you. When you fall down, dust yourself off and keep going. Perseverance, fortitude, resolve, bravery, and conviction are your battle cry! You have renewed confidence with every hardship you encounter. Your courage and self confidence is on the rise, as you are riding a new wave in order to weather all storms. You find your truest self and become the man or woman that thirsts for greatness. The Spirit lifts you and you are soaring, you are roaring, you are everything that God had foreseen when He chose you. You pick up your cross daily and fight for another day. Your toughness, steadiness, and power is intense. Your trust and faith has grown supremely. People around you cannot stop and not notice.

This is the life you have desired all along. Your hunger within you craved for this chance. You worked, sacrificed, were disciplined, and battled to make it happen. You decided in your mind to choose a new path, to have laser sharp focus and elicit that tunnel vision. Nothing and no one will be able to stop you. You are untamed, you are holy, you are a saint in the making. Your life is a living testimony and the greatest witness. Your fervor and zeal, your zest and willingness to go after it and hunt it down is changing your lot in life. You no longer make excuses, you find solutions and continue to do whatever it takes. You are now living your best life. The joy, inner peace, and happiness that flows inside you is unlike anything you have ever experienced and the best part is that it will never subside. It is not fleeting and will last forever. You can be sure of this because you have changed the game. You have allowed Christ in and the very power that raised Him from the dead, the very spirit that brought Jesus to new life, is living inside of you. You know who you are and most importantly, you know to whom you belong! You are a child of God and a descendent of the most high. "No, in all these things we conquer overwhelmingly through him who loved us. For I am convinced that neither death, nor life, nor angels, nor principalities, nor present things, nor future things, nor powers, nor height, nor depth, nor any other creature will be able to separate us from the love of God in Christ Jesus our Lord." (Romans 8:37-39)

You are a king. You are a queen. You have been crowned with life. Your ultimate throne awaits you at the end of the age. You are spectacular and magnificent. You are shining and dazzling, clothed with incredible brilliance and light. Your radiance and heart is illuminating profoundly, as you are a beacon of light glistening for all to see. The fire that blazes inside of you cannot and will never burn out. As Jennifer Herndon reminds us, "The smallest spark ignites the fire that lies deep inside you, and suddenly everything is possible." Each of us has that fire that burns within the very core of our being. For some of us it is already blazing, roaring and red hot. For others it is an ember, a small flicker of light. The rest of humanity falls somewhere in between. Regardless of the size of our flame today, we can be reignited and blaze within. The fire in our hearts can be stoked to scorch a path of victory for our lives, while incinerating a trail that changes the world. It is time for you to live out the very words of St. Paul and continue to heed them as your song, "I have fought the good fight, I have finished the race, I have kept the faith. Now there is in store for me the crown of righteousness, which the

Lord, the righteous Judge, will award to me on that day—and not only to me, but also to all who have longed for his appearing." (2 Timothy 4:7-8)

You have been crowned today and you will wear this crown until you wear it anew when you cross the ultimate finish line. The gates of Heaven will welcome you, but as for now you continue to run. You remain on track and your ardor is greater than ever. Now, you not only run for yourself, but you run as a shining example to the world. You have relayed this great message of hope to all, and there are others now running beside you. Your eyes are fixated on the prize! You have claimed your crown and in your own way, your life has expressed to others that victory is theirs for the taking!

"What you wish to ignite in others, must first burn within yourself." -Marc Accetta

Author's Note

I wanted to take a moment to articulate the amount of satisfaction I had in writing this book. As an English Language Arts teacher for nearly a decade, as an avid reader, and being someone who seeks inspiration, I have read hundreds of works of literature. This process has instilled in me a newfound respect for each and every author as it is a tall task to compile one's ideas to the confines of a page. It is with great pleasure that I had this opportunity to write down my personal thoughts, feelings, and beliefs. I have enjoyed sharing with you my story and what has lit the fire inside of me that continues to burn brightly and fiercely. There have been so many life experiences, God moments, challenges, and life lessons along the way.

My hope is that you were able to get something positive out of this book and are able to feel more encouraged and inspired. My goal with the stories that I shared from my personal life and those of people who I admire and look up to, was to show you that no matter what stage of life you are in or what you face, you can overcome it. Never stop and as Dean Karnazes said so well, "run when you can, walk if you have to, crawl if you must; just never give up." There is a fire burning within you, set it ablaze! You have what it takes and the life you yearn and long for can be yours!

It is my desire that the tips, strategies, suggestions, and gameplan that was laid out for you, along with a well balanced life anchored on faith, can lead you to become someone you are proud of when you look in the mirror each day. My hope is that in time we might see the challenges we face in a new way as they build our characters and make us stronger version of ourselves: "but we rejoice in our sufferings, knowing that suffering produces endurance, and endurance produces character, and character produces hope, and hope does not put us to shame, because God's love has been poured into our hearts through the Holy Spirit who has been given to us." (Romans 5:3-5)

Life is hard. Despite the difficulties and darkness that looms in our world, there is so much light. There is much more beauty and goodness in you and for you to experience. Know that I am praying for you and am truly grateful that you have taken precious time out of your day and life to read this book. May God bless you and know that you have everything inside of you to be a true champion in this life and in the world to come. Your crown is there for the taking!

To close, you will find on the following pages some of my favorite and most encouraging Bible verses and scriptures. I hope that they inspire you as much as they have inspired and carried me. Read them often and know that God's army is behind you every step of the way!

Scripture for Encouragement

I wanted to share with you some of my favorite bible verses to encourage you along the way. Read them daily and often to put some wind back in your sails. As you allow this scripture to sink in and you pray with it, know that God has your back and we are praying for you. God bless you.

"Cast all your anxiety on him because he cares for you." (1 Peter 5:7)

"For my thoughts are not your thoughts, neither are your ways my ways,'declares the Lord.' As the heavens are higher than the earth, so are my ways higher than your ways and my thoughts than your thoughts.'" (Isaiah 55:8-9)

"Give me your heart...and let your eyes delight in my ways." (Proverbs 23:26)

"You brought us to a place of abundance." (Psalms 66:12)

"I came so that you might have life and have it more abundantly... have it to the full." (John 10:10)

"For we are God's workmanship, created in Christ Jesus to do good works, which God prepared in advance for us to do." (Ephesians 2:10)

"Come unto me, all ye that labour and are heavy laden, and I will give you rest. Take my yoke upon you, and learn of me; for I am meek and lowly in heart: and ye shall find rest unto your souls. For my yoke is easy, and my burden is light" (Matthew 11:28-31)

"The way of the righteous is like the first gleam of dawn, which shines ever brighter until the full light of day." (Proverbs 4:18)

"Cast your cares on the LORD and he will sustain you; he will never let the righteous fall." (Psalm 55:22)

"Cast all your anxiety on him because he cares for you." (1 Peter 5:7)

"You are my refuge and my shield; I have put my hope in your word. Away from me, you evildoers, that I may keep the commands of my God!" (Psalm 119:114-115)

"My comfort in my suffering is this: Your promise preserves my life." (Psalm 119:50)

"I call on the LORD in my distress, and he answers me." (Psalm 120:1)

"Many are saying of me, "God will not deliver him." "Selah" But you are a shield around me, O LORD; you bestow glory on me and lift up my head. To the LORD I cry aloud, and he answers me from his holy hill. "Selah" I lie down and sleep; I wake again, because the LORD sustains me. I will not fear the tens of thousands drawn up against me on every side." (Psalm 3:2-6)

"Joshua said to them, "Do not be afraid; do not be discouraged. Be strong and courageous. This is what the LORD will do to all the enemies you are going to fight." (Joshua 10:25)

"Praise be to the God and Father of our Lord Jesus Christ! In his great mercy he has given us new birth into a living hope through the resurrection of Jesus Christ from the dead, and into an inheritance that can never perish, spoil or fade—kept in heaven for you, who through faith are shielded by God's power until the coming of the salvation that is ready to be revealed in the last time. In this you greatly rejoice, though now for a little while you may have had to suffer grief in all kinds of trials." (1 Peter 1:3-6)

"You will be secure, because there is hope; you will look about you and take your rest in safety. You will lie down, with no one to make you afraid, and many will court your favor." (Job 11:18-19)

"...through whom we have gained access by faith into this grace in which we now stand. And we rejoice in the hope of the glory of God. Not only so, but we also rejoice in our sufferings, because we know that suffering produces perseverance; perseverance, character; and character, hope. And hope does not disappoint us, because God has poured out his love into our hearts by the Holy Spirit, whom he has given us. You see, at just the right time, when we were still powerless, Christ died for the ungodly. Very rarely will anyone die for a righteous man, though for a good man someone might possibly dare to die." (Romans 5:2-7)

"I can do everything through Christ who gives me strength." (Philippians 4:13)

"He gives strength to the weary and increases the power of the weak." (Isaiah 40:29)

"My soul is weary with sorrow; strengthen me according to your word." (Psalm 119:28)

"but those who hope in the LORD will renew their strength. They will soar on wings like eagles; they will run and not grow weary, they will walk and not be faint." (Isaiah 40:31)

"God is our refuge and strength, an ever-present help in trouble." (Psalm 46:1)

"The LORD is my strength and my shield; my heart trusts in him, and I am helped. My heart leaps for joy and I will give thanks to him in song. The LORD is the strength of his people, a fortress of salvation for his anointed one." (Psalm 28:7-8)

"O LORD, be gracious to us; we long for you. Be our strength every morning, our salvation in time of distress." (Isaiah 33:2)

"He gives strength to the weary and increases the power of the weak. Even youths grow tired and weary, and young men stumble and fall; but those who hope in the LORD will renew their strength. They will soar on wings like eagles; they will run and not grow weary, they will walk and not be faint." (Isaiah 40:29-31)

"I pray that out of his glorious riches he may strengthen you with power through his Spirit in your inner being," (Ephesians 3:16)

"Fear not [there is nothing to fear], for I am with you...I will help you; yes, I will hold you up and retain you with My [victorious] right hand..." (Isaiah 41:10)

"For I know the plans that I have for you," declares the Lord, ``plans to prosper you and not to harm you, plans to give you hope and a future." (Jeremiah 29:11)

"I have told you these things so that my joy might be in you and your joy might be complete." (John 15:11)

"I will never leave you or forsake you." (Hebrews 13:5)

"But if God so clothes the grass of the field, which today is alive and tomorrow is thrown into the oven, will he not much more clothe you, O you of little faith?" (Matthew 6:30)

"The way of the righteous is like the first gleam of dawn, which shines ever brighter until the full light of day." (Proverbs 4:18)

"For God hath not given us the spirit of fear; but of power, and of love, and of a sound mind." (2 Timothy 1:7)

"So do not fear, for I am with you; do not be dismayed, for I am your God. I will strengthen you and help you; I will uphold you with my righteous right hand." (Isaiah 41:10)

For we are God's workmanship, created in Christ Jesus to do good works, which God prepared in advance for us to do. (Ephesians 2:10)

"Come unto me, all ye that labour and are heavy laden, and I will give you rest. Take my yoke upon you, and learn of me; for I am meek and lowly in heart: and ye shall find rest unto your souls. For my yoke is easy, and my burden is light." (Matthew 11:28-31)

"Trust in the LORD with all your heart and lean not on your own understanding; in all your ways acknowledge him, and he will make your paths straight." (Proverbs 3:5-6)

"Teach us to number our days, that we may gain a heart of wisdom." (Psalm 90:12)

"Peace I leave with you; my peace I give you. I do not give to you as the world gives. Do not let your hearts be troubled and do not be afraid." (John 14:27)

"I have told you these things, so that in me you may have peace. In this world you will have trouble. But take heart! I have overcome the world." (John 16:33)

"God is our refuge and strength, an ever-present help in trouble. Therefore we will not fear, though the earth give way and the mountains fall into the heart of the sea, though its waters roar and foam and the mountains quake with their surging." (Psalm 46:1-3)

References

Doyle, Glennon. *Untamed*, The Dial Press: New York, New York. 2020.

Goggins, David. *Can't Hurt Me: Master Your Mind and Defy the Odds*, David Goggins Publications, 2018.

Osteen, Joel. *Blessed in the Darkness*, Faith Publisher: Philadelphia, Pennsylvania, 2017.

Osteen, Joel. "Change the Channel Sermon," Joel Osteen Ministries, Houston, Texas, 2013.

Thomas, Eric. *Greatness is Upon You*, Eric Thomas and Associates Publications, 2013.

Tolle, Eckhart. *A New Earth*, The Dutton/Penguin Group: Westminster, England, 2005.

Tolle, Eckhart. *The Power of NOW*, Namaste Publishing: Vancouver, Canada, 1997.

Vitale, Dick. *Living the Dream*, Sports Publishing LLC: Chicago, Illinois, 2003.

Willinick, Jacko & Babin, Leif. Extreme Ownership, St. Martin's Press: New York, New York, 2017.